BOSTON'S BEST
DIVE BARS

BOSTON'S BEST DIVE BARS

Drinking and Diving in Beantown

LUKE O'NEIL

Brooklyn, New York

Printed in the USA
10 9 8 7 6 5 4 3 2 1

Gamble Guides is an imprint of
Ig Publishing
392 Clinton Avenue
Brooklyn, NY 11238
www.igpub.com

Author photo by Michelle Crowley

ISBN: 978-1-935439-25-7

DELIVERY

TO:

Route To:

Date: 02/19/2016

For: Athol Public Library
568 Main St.
Athol, MA 01331
USA

Pick up: Athol Public Library

FROM:

Boston Public Library - West Roxbury Branch

Due: 4/16/2016 4:59:59 AM

Notes:

Athol
Public Library
568 Main St., Athol MA 01331

You checked out the following item(s):

1. **Boston's best dive bars : drinking and diving in Beantown**, No Circ Modifier Applied : No Circ Modifier Applied : no circ modifier applied by O'Neil, Luke.
   Due: **3/28/16 11:59 PM**
   Barcode: 39999068159944

M, W, Th, F 9:30am - 5:30pm
Tues 9:30am - 8:00pm

Call us at (978) 249-9515
Visit us online at www.athollibrary.org

You saved: $0.00 by coming to the Athol Public Library!

Athol
Public Library

568 Main St. Athol MA 01331

You checked out the following item(s)

1. **Boston's best dive bars : drinking and diving in Beantown.** No One Modifier Applied - no one modifier applied by O'Neil, Luke.
   Due 3/28/16 11:59 PM
   Barcode: 32990081366041

M W Th F 9:30am - 5:30pm
Tue-S 30am- 8:00pm

Call us at (978) 249-0515
Visit us online at www.atholibrary.org

You saved: $0.00 by coming to the Athol Public Library!

Thanks to my friends for being such knowledgeable alcoholics (but, you know, the cute kind), and to Michelle, for always letting me steal all her ideas.

Boston's Best Dive Bars
(arranged by neighborhood)

ALLSTON/BRIGHTON/BROOKLINE
The Boyne Pub
Bus Stop Pub
Hogan's Run
Joey's
The Last Drop
The Model Café
Silhouette Lounge

BOSTON
Anchovies
The Bar Room
Beacon Hill Pub
Biddy Early's
Black Horse Tavern
Corner Pub
Delux Cafe
The Dugout
The Eagle
JJ Donovan's
JJ Foley's
The Penalty Box
Punter's Pub
Red Hat Cafe
Remmingtons
Shangrilla Chinese Restaurant
Side Bar
Sullivan's Tap
The Tam
TC's Lounge
Wally's Cafe

CAMBRIDGE
The Cantab Lounge
Charlie's Kitchen
Courtside Restaurant and Pub
Joey Mac's
Newtowne Grille
Paddy's Lunch
Portugalia
Pugliese Bar & Grill
Riverside Pizza
Whitney's Cafe

CHARLESTOWN/NORTH END
Corner Cafe
Durty Nelly's
Four Winds Bar and Grille
Old Sully's
Sullivan's Pub
Tavern At the End of the World

DORCHESTER
Centre Bar
The Dot Tavern
Dublin House
The Eire Pub
Lower Mills Pub
Sonny's Adams
Tom English Bar
Twelve Bens
Upstairs Downstairs

EAST BOSTON/CHELSEA

Chelsea Walk Pub
Eddie C's
Parrotta's Alpine Lodge
Taverna Medallo
Trainor's Cafe
Victory Pub

JAMAICA PLAIN/
ROSLINDALE

BK's
Cottage Tavern
The Drinking Fountain
Galway House
JJ Foley's Fireside Tavern
Midway Cafe
Robyn's Bar and Grill

ROXBURY

Aga's Highland Tap
El Mondonguito
Pat "Packy" Connors Tavern

SOMERVILLE

Casey's
Fasika
On the Hill Tavern
The Pub
P.A.'s Lounge
Rosebud Bar and Grill
Sligo Pub

SOUTH BOSTON

Ace's High
The Connection
The Corner Tavern
Cornerstone Pub
Croke Park/ Whitey's
Kiley's Tavern
Murphy's Law
Quencher Tavern
Touchie's Shamrock Pub
Tom English's Cottage
The Shannon Tavern
Shea's Tavern
Williams Tavern

Introduction

A dive bar is a series of contradictions. It's usually an objectively bad bar in terms of service, product, and décor, but it's also the best bar you know. It's a place where you might recognize all the regulars, but one where you can drink in piece and blend into the scenery without anyone casting judgment.

A dive bar can simultaneously be the regular haunt of college-age kids getting their first taste of the drinking world as well as the old-timers who've spent fifty years in the same stool. It's a bar colored by the demographics of the neighborhood it's in, particularly in the still relatively segregated but rapidly gentrifying parts of Boston, but also a place where certain time-honored traditions hold fast. A dive is a bar where literally anything and everything can happen on any given night, but more often than not the predictable patterns of inertia rule.

Over the course of the past year I spent researching this book (getting drunk, in other words), I found roughly 120 different bars that fit that description. We've had to omit some of them for space, but an equal number of them have closed since I began. That's a pattern that doesn't seem likely to change any time soon as real estate prices continue to climb, and many of the people who built these bars, either literally, or through their decades-long patronage, die off or are priced out of the neighborhoods. I wouldn't be surprised if a few more included here have gone under while this book goes to print. That's emblematic of the biggest contradiction that a dive embodies: it's a bar that has somehow withstood the test of time, but isn't long for the changing world.

Rating System

🍾 Fun for the whole family.

🍾🍾 I wouldn't bring my mother here. Yours maybe.

🍾🍾🍾 Nice place. For a dump.

🍾🍾🍾🍾 You could get stabbed, but you'd have to work for it.

🍾🍾🍾🍾🍾 A wretched hive of scum and villainy. Welcome home.

Best Dive Bars, college kids and hipsters version
Ace's High
Beacon Hill Pub
The Cantab Lounge
Punter's Pub
Silhouette Lounge
Sligo Pub
The Courtside Restaurant and Pub
Delux Café
The Tam
Wally's Cafe
TC's Lounge

Best Dive Bars, townies and old-timers version
BK's
Paddy's Lunch
Parrotta's Alpine Lodge
Quencher Tavern
Pat "Packy" Connors Tavern
Croke Park/ Whitey's
The Dot Tavern
The Drinking Fountain
Hogan's Run
Old Sully's

Bus Stop Pub

ALLSTON/BRIGHTON/ BROOKLINE

The Boyne Pub

458 Western Ave., Brighton
Phone: 617-782-2418

Dive Bar Rating

This plump little fortress of an Irish pub appears out of nowhere on a shady, desolate stretch of Western Ave., home to vaguely fascist looking science labs (or something, who can even tell,) and sketchy auto body shops. While it may have undergone a renovation a few years back with a bright tin roof installed, dark stained wooden trimmings and a rich yellow paint job, it's a good example of how in many cases all the gentrification of a dive bar does is give old townies a nicer looking room in which to drink away the afternoon. A dive is more a state of mind than a place anyway.

The Boyne takes its name from a significant waterway in Irish history; its likeness is frosted onto the mirror behind the bar. It was the site of a famous battle between the Catholic King James and the Protestant King William, two rivals for the throne in 1690. William won, incidentally, and Protestant rule ensued. None of that tribal horseshit seems to be on anyone's mind when I pass through here though. I'm certainly not stupid enough to bring it up anyway. Rivalries of a more recent vintage preoccupy the convivial group of European track suit-wearing rogues and XXL Patriots jersey-sporting regulars. There's a collection for the NFL betting pool going on at the bar. I'm tempted to throw in, but the last thing I need is another way to lose money on football. It's nice to see Irish guys give a shit about real football for a change.

It's not always so peaceful though. Last year three mopes were arrested in a brief struggle with undercover cops for carrying loaded hand guns. One of them tried ditching the piece in the trash can in the bathroom during the melee. Somehow that move never works out.

"I saw a total bloodbath fight there once," my friend who comes here a lot told me. "A guy got his head split by a glass or something. I never went back. There was blood everywhere. But I was able to score some charlie here the same night before the townie fisticuffs." Well, there's a positive ending to every tale I guess.

Thankfully there's no dirt going down when I stop in. The internet jukebox in the corner is keeping the room bouncing in a bizarre, but surprisingly apt mix of Daft Punk and Sinatra.

"It's a mix, it really is," the Irish bartender says of the crowd here. "It's all ages from twenty one up. You get some older fellers," she says, nodding to the group over by the taps and lowering her voice. "But they usually just stand by the bar while the young girls go off and dance."

"You know a dive when you hit the door," says Rob Potylo, the Boston musician and comedian better known as his alter ego Robby Roadsteamer. "There are bars people drink at to be seen, and there are bars that you just want to 'dive' under a stool and let Mr. Booze take over. I like the Boyne because it has amazing food, and great bartenders, but it still feels like a dive. There's always a divey type fella at the bar and it never seems too busy. I'm sure hipsters have already hit it once or twice and shit on it and left. They usually stay on the Deep Ellum, Model side of the tracks in the Allston area. Hipsters don't like walking too far to get fucked up." They should get out more.

Bus Stop Pub

252 Western Avenue., Allston.
Phone: 617-254-4086

Dive Bar Rating

"Welcome to Narnia" writes one online reviewer of this Allston dive. It's true, this classic is most certainly a magical crossroads of sorts, both literally and figuratively speaking. Out front on busy Western Ave. you'll find groups of young mothers wrangling their bundled children side by side with Allston twenty-somethings all waiting for the #86 or #70 with the impatient purgatory-like glaze that street side bus stops engender. But the bar's location on the borderline between the vast grassy playing fields surrounding the ancient colosseum edifice of Harvard Stadium and the dense residential sprawl of Allston's immigrant and student communities hammer the crossroads metaphor home. This neighborhood is ground zero for the University's omnivorous real estate grab, a perpetual thorn in town vs. gown grievances.

The proximity to some of the graduate schools also makes the bar a worthy stop off for slumming B-school assholes in training. More likely you'll find post-college types rubbing dirty elbows with locals and piling in for games of flip cup after a flag football or frisbee game.

For years this was a watering spot for local TV crews as well, a friend in the industry who asked me not to use his name says. "We used to go get all surly after work with the surly waitresses and watch as the satellite truck drivers from WBZ would show up in all their glory before work and drink alongside the b-list news personalities and the management who hung out there, god knows why, after work."

On a snow-covered Saturday it's just a jovial crew of regulars riding out the storm inside. It looks like a ski lodge in here, with a sloping roof, mounted taxidermy and slatted wooden benches. A couple of kids are eating fried cheese at one corner of the bar next to a group playing touch screen games. "I don't like it here," my girlfriend says instantly. She'll change her mind by the end of our stay though.

"I imagine someone trying to be festive putting those up," she says, pointing out the half-hearted Christmas decorations. "It's depressing."

No surprise, the Keno business seems to be chugging along pretty steadily today. "Someone should write a story about the way the Keno industry preys on alcoholics." That's why you don't bring your girlfriend to a dive, by the way. No offense to girlfriends.

A sloppy Irish guy wobbles over and asks to try on my glasses. We're not sure if he wants to be friends or punch me out. He probably isn't sure either. Hard to tell with Irish drunks, they're exactly 50% menace and 50% jovial. Turns out he just wanted to complain about his pregnant wife and mother in law. "Why do I pay for a place for them to eat, sleep and shit, and yet somehow I'm not good enough?" That right there is probably the single most frequently asked question running through the minds of the type of guys you find drinking in dive bars across the city on any afternoon.

Our attention turns to the long murals along either wall, a dense grouping of caricatures painted one on top of the next. "Some are famous people. A lot of them are old regulars," says Devin the bartender.

"You can tell they're all pretty old if you get a look at their duds. Some come in still, but they're barely recognizable. It's been years since the artist who did them has come in, but from what I hear customers would drop him like ten or fifteen bucks and he'd have them up on the wall in twenty minutes. If you look over in the corner there are some sketches that he never got around to finishing."

They're more like ghostly outlines of long lost regulars. Every dive bar has those, just not literally like this. As time goes by, the memories, and the customers fade.

Later on that night we see our friend the henpecked husband stumbling home to his tyrannical mother in law in the cold. It's snowing hard now, so it's hard to make him out clearly. One second he's there, the next he's fading away.

Hogan's Run

8 Lincoln St., Brighton
Phone: 617-254-9407

Dive Bar Rating

"Time stands still at Hogan's Run." It's a common refrain I heard when asking people about their impression of this classic tiny brick dive sitting on a largely forgotten block overlooking the Mass Pike that looks like the edge of the known universe. That can mean one of two things. In one sense the bar is a throwback, old man watering hole that progress seems to have forgotten. On the other, its early 8 a.m. opening hour, lack of windows, and steady day time business means it's possible to lose an entire day drinking here without even realizing it.

The new WGBH public radio and television studios nearby, as well as the New Balance complex, should in theory be injecting more life blood into the bar, but it's by and large populated by grimy locals. They tried booking rock shows here a few different times over the years, but it hasn't taken off.

"It's your classic shit hole," one regular who didn't want to be identified explained. "Basically a last resort bar for people who have been kicked out of everywhere else now. It's owned by a real winner. There is some better clientèle that roll through, but their bread and butter is mainly the coke and Keno set."

"Everyone says that it's the place where people go that have been kicked out of everywhere else," a second regular told me. "But it's not true at all."

"Okay it is," he admitted later. "But people other than that go there. Last night there were some New Balance people there, then some locals, and even some younger 'normals.' They are slowly getting a better clientele. A major crackdown happened a year or two ago and it's now mostly on the Keno end from what I hear and see. Not a bad place to go on a weeknight if you want cheap drinks and to ignore the world."

The drinkers all seemed jittery when I lurked into the quiet room on a Saturday. The crowd was friendly enough—to one another. Everyone here is a recurring character in everyone else's boozy narrative. I might as well have not existed. Or perhaps I existed so thoroughly it was blowing people's minds.

It's much busier in the morning, Kevin the bartender told me, asking my name. Introducing yourself is twofold in a place like this. Everyone else knows each other already, so it makes sense. But it's also a matter of "Well, who the fuck are you anyway?" I felt like I'd just crashed a wedding with a clown suit on.

They get a lot of guys coming in after working the over night shift. Seems a more likely crowd than the public radio types nipping in for a glass of Sauvignon Blanc. There's a band rehearsal studio around the corner from here that brings in a slow stream of straggly Allston rockers as well. Cheap beer, busy bathrooms, and a general sense of cultural isolation are the hallmarks of a good dive. They've got all that in spades here.

Joey's

416 Market St., Brighton.
Phone: 617-254-9381

Dive Bar Rating

Is it weird to be turned on by a forty year old 1980s hair metal babe in ripped, acid wash cutoffs with an Irish brogue, who's fighting valiantly against the push back from her coked-out brain as she tries to order a round of beers, then pay for them, then carry them back to her table? Because if so, I should probably go talk to somebody. A sniffling, vacant-eyed bonny lass like this is a good example of how sometimes it's more the people that make the dive, as opposed to the look of the bar itself. I had my doubts about including this Oak Square pub on the list when I was roaming through the bar-heavy neighborhood of Brighton, but all that changed when I came across Kelly and her friends. The rest of the lot wasn't much to look at either; all sour pusses and grim glares from bikers, construction workers and fat dudes in low-riding Sox caps. Even the bartender seemed annoyed that he had to leave his dart game to come ask me what I'm having.

In other words, pay no attention to the remodeling done in here. You can't paint over an attitude. With a few minor subtractions, in terms of décor, and clientele, this might be able to pass for a trendy city bar. But as it is, with its thick sheen of fresh black paint on the walls and ceiling, and the dim track lighting, it's like an avant-garde box theater where they're staging a production of some German nihilist deconstruction of ennui. Put this bar downtown and it would be selling $16 martinis. Put it in Providence and it would be a strip club; the way the lights fall on the bar it looks a lot like a cat walk for pros working the room.

With so many other bars around here, the owners must have figured it was time to get their act together and fall into line with the prevalent upscale Irish pub look. But they forgot to raise their prices, and they forgot about neighborhood drinkers' brand loyalty. Good, I say. Porter Belly's and the Green Briar, and the Brighton Beer Garden and Devlin's and the Corrib are all right around the way if you don't like to take a little cheek with your pint. Each of those have their own charms, but how many of them have a roll of scratch tickets dangling behind the bar, or Cheezits for sale, or Keno, or an over-sized Golden Tea video console? Or slutty extras from Sons of Anarchy working the juke? With so many other options, Joey's doesn't get nearly as crowded as the other bars around here on the weekends. If you're over here and you want a more low key place to swill cheap beer, this is your best bet.

They don't serve any food either, which is always a plus in my estimation. Who wants to get drunk with the smell of fried cheese and grease in the air? But they do serve a really loud juke box. That helps to get the Irish girls grinding like zombies to "Sweet Child of Mine." Young Axl would've pissed on this place probably, it's not dive enough for that legend of fuckery, but the strip club staple feels just right in here. "Where do we go now?" No idea. Stay here till they make us leave I suppose. The lights are reflecting off the dark polished bar just right, the music is blaring, and at least some of the crowd is really feeling it. Really feeling something anyway. Like I said, sometimes it's not the paint on the walls that makes a dive, it's the paint chips in the customer's nostrils.

(Kelsey Marie Bell)

The Last Drop

596 Washington St., Brighton
Phone:617-787-1111

The name here is cute, but it's also meant to be taken literally. One of the only spots in the area open until 2 a.m., despite the abundance of bars, this is the one the kids head to at 1:30 for their last drop of booze. The one they really, definitely need and isn't going to make them feel like shit the next day.

People come earlier in the night as well. During the school year it's not unusual to see a line out the door on weekends made up of BC students anxious to yell into each other's faces on the dance floor of sorts. The exposed brick walls, pipes and vents, and the virtual lack of tables in the room give it a hangar-like feel. "It feels like a firehouse in the off hours," my friend Erik said last time we came in.

When the room isn't full it smells like popcorn. They don't serve food, but they'll put out bowls of the salty stuff to whet your drinking boner. In that respect, and in their early opening time at noon, the bar hues toward the divey neighborhood end. Old timers and laborers fuck off for a quick wet lunch in here on their breaks; the High Lifes are only $2.50. That's good news for you, but I'm gonna pass on that flat piss champagne myself. Make mine a Maker's Mark here, I say to the bartender, who checks my ID promptly. That should probably tell you something about how worried they are about underage drinking if you know what I look like. Flip to the back of the book I guess. No way that guy is anywhere near 21.

Like the Castlebar across the street, this place was shined up a few years ago. The ceilings were raised and covered in tin, and the facade was given an eye-watering coat of Irish-red paint. The brick walls toward the pool tables are covered in names and scores written in chalk though, and the bathrooms look like a Greyhound bus shitter.

All in all it's rather a simulacrum of a dive bar, but it's close enough to the reality to trick you anyway. It's the type of place you go by day to flirt with the townie-hot bartender, or to have a beer while you're doing your laundry next door like the patron who'd snuck away from his whites in the cycle to nip in for a pint. "I used to come here all the time when I lived in the neighborhood," he said. He was wearing a Patriots jersey, sitting beneath a Patriots banner, reading about the Patriots in the newspaper. "It's an everyone is welcome place. A great neighborhood bar, it's not a scene." Further hammering home his home team bona fides, he summed up the appeal of The Last Drop with Belichick-like concision. "It is," he said, "what it is."

What that is exactly probably depends on who you are—a quiet drinker looking to relax in a no-frills, cheap dive-pub environment, or a bro-hammer looking to stand in the throng of douches long enough that some drunk BC chick will agree to take you home for a dry hand job. Pick your poison.

(Kelsey Marie Bell)

The Model Cafe

7 North Beacon St., Allston
Phone: 617-254-9365

Dive Bar Rating

For as long as I can remember, and I've been drinking in Boston for about a decade now, the Model has always been the centerpiece of the rock and roll hub of Allston's rugged youth bar scene. The place where aging local rockers and the younger versions of themselves come to catch last call post-rock show at one of the many clubs around the way. Or the first stop of a boozy night for the type of scenesters who live together in seven bedroom flophouses with clogged bathtubs and post-hurricane destruction level décor. Maybe that was just me though.

In the past few years they've made an effort to bring DJ nights and such in, to give people a musical genre theme to do their drinking to. Allstonites live for that sort of synergy. I asked Sean Drinkwater, a musician from Boston synthpop heroes Freezepop who's been coming here forever about how it's changed over the years. If anyone's an expert on the Model, it would be him.

"I guess there is an implied lack of pretense at a place like the Model," he told me. "That's a dive, right? When I walk in there wearing some quasi-80's fashion disaster, I am generally the only one."

It has changed a bit though. "Every now and again they spend a few dollars on a new couch or some odd lighting fixture, but you still basically know that you're at the Model and your expectations of the experience are probably going to be fulfilled. Granted said expectations are probably not exactly lofty in the first place.

The typical night there, he says, is a loud one. Most of the crew has probably damaged their hearing from years of show-going or practice space sonic assault. "It's earplug-worthy recently, which sets it apart from the Silhouette or a similar kind of place. It is usually a mix of metal heads, punk kids and indie-rockers with a few assorted randoms. Over the years it's become a bit more mellow. When the smoking ban went into effect it did seem to hurt the energy of the place for a long time, but they're slowly getting back to where they were. I would say in the late nineties it was certainly a more rough establishment. The patrons had more opportunities for bodily injury back then. Now it's just the staff that ends up having swings taken at them usually."

Despite that, or because of that actually, it's always been a hotspot for indie rock personalities for some reason, he says. Robert Smith and the Dandy Warhols being maybe two of the more well-known examples to have strutted through on my watch. "My own strange experience there was hanging out with Bauhaus/Love and Rockets guitarist Daniel Ash after he played a solo show at the Paradise," Drinkwater says. "A few of us ended up back on his bus listening to *Violator* which was surreal and kind of perfect for me. Another odd experience was seeing my very recent ex-girlfriend hook up with the drummer from Jesus Jones. That doesn't happen every day. I don't think?"

No, but if it was gonna happen anywhere it would probably be here.

Silhouette Lounge

200 Brighton Ave., Allston
Phone: 617-254-9306

Dive Bar Rating

Cease your searching weary dive traveller. At long last you've come home. All is well now. Close your eyes, picture the dive of your dreams—beat up regulars soused on cheap beer, free popcorn behind the bar, darts, pool, scratch tickets, juke box, Golden Tee, Buck Hunter, Christmas lights dangling from the ceilings, faux wood finishing, horror-show bathrooms—it's all here. Home sweet home. Probably the platonic ideal of the Allston dive, the Silly, as they call it, is the collision of slummy Allston's two competing biological species: the twenty something scenester, and the grizzled old alcoholic, both of whom populate this diverse dive ecosystem in all of their shit-faced splendor. The only difference of course, is that it's cute when you're a fresh twenty three year old just dipping your healthy pink noses into the beery froth of the city's bar culture every night of the week. When you're a wobbly old-timer with nothing left to lose, not so much. On any given night it's like watching the young'ins drink in harmony with future version of themselves. Just like an episode of Lost in a way. The kids are just the flashbacks running concurrently with the rundown, beaten up castaways on a scary island.

My own backstory features quite a few episodes here as well. Last ditch attempts at making something (good or bad) of the night before it was time to trudge off to some goofy, over-crowded, under-supplied house party. I'm a lot more mature now of course. I do my dive drinking well before midnight.

"I think it is the best example of a dive bar," my friend Mike, a musician who lives around the corner tells me. "When I go there I throw my name up on the pool board, pick like ten jams from the music box and drill pops with whatever crew I'm with. There's a sweet fenced in back area to smoke too, random townie regulars... everything you need. Also, the best popcorn in the world."

I went back to remind myself the other night. God, he's right. Something about that sweet buttery salt that makes the cheap beer go down perfectly. I start flashing back to more rugged times in here before long though. It's filled with aging hipsters. With my glasses off the people appear blurry with all the signifiers of Allston bar youth—army coats, long hair, weird hats, nose rings—but look closer at their faces and the wrinkles beneath the costume are showing through.

Courtney Cox, an editor at the *Weekly Dig*, swears by the place as well. "The Silly's my favorite bar in Boston because of the crowd,' she tells me. "The dart leaguers stay after their matches and teach newbies how to play, the bartenders tease you for months about the night you had one too many, and though I'd be totally wary of most of the regulars in real life, everyone's cool with everyone else inside. Most area bars have had their longtime regular crowd driven out by college kids, but at The Silhouette, the regulars still rule." The irregulars too.

An interview with James Lynch of the Dropkick Murphys

The Dropkick Murphys are pretty much the embodiment of Boston bar culture in musical form. I asked James Lynch, guitarist in the band, about his favorite dives in the city.

So what do you think makes a dive bar a dive?

I think a dive bar is more a family environment than just any other bar you pop into you know what I mean? My favorite dive bar was O'Malleys in Union Square in Allston. It was the closest thing to a second family I had. You know who is gonna be there every night. You know exactly what's gonna happen. You have your drink waiting for you on the bar, you know what's gonna be on the TV.

That place closed in 2003, right?

Yeah, and me and the rest of the regulars scurried across the street to the Silhouette at that point. A neighborhood bar is an institution. Like I said, it's like a family thing, and once it's gone, it's gone. The place that took over where O'Malley's [Deep Ellum] used to be couldn't be any less of a dive bar.

Do you think eventually all the character is going to be gone from Allston at some point?

I certainly hope not. My wife owns a tattoo shop on Harvard Ave, so we've been right in the middle of it watching it disappear. All the places that have been there forever, Marty's Liquors, Economy Hardware... are gone. The streets are getting vacant. People can't afford to pay the rent out there anymore. As more of those little businesses disappear, the more the personality of the area goes right with it.

The tattoo shop is right near O'Briens. That used to be a real shitty dive rock venue. Now it looks kind of nice.

I still like going in there because it's still O'Briens. I always joke that it looks they bought one of those bathroom refinishing kits and just put it over the old O'Briens. You know what's still in there, and you know it's the same joint, it's just got a prettier face on it. I think they tried to make up for the old bathroom by making a wicked nice bathroom.

What other spots do the band like?
We love TC's Lounge down off of Mass Ave. Once again, it's a classic dive. It's dark in there, they've got pinball, it's just a good place to sit in the corner and be left alone.

Do you think TC's or the Sillhouette are good examples of an ironic dive, where the kids are like "Hey look at us! We're in a dive bar!"?
The day I turned 21 I went to the Sill. Some people are attracted to it. You can tell the people that are there because they think it's ironic and the people that are there because it's home. I see people on a regular basis come in and be like "Oh look at this place!" Like it's a novelty. I definitely think there's that crowd. That crowd might be the people that are keeping the places open.

Family businesses like a lot of these dives are hard to keep open these days.
If everyone in there is drinking on the cuff then no one's gonna make any money.

Has Boston's bar culture changed since the band first started out?
It's changed without question. We were just talking about Kenmore Square. The band started at the Rat. That's a perfect example of how dramatically everything has changed. It's a completely different place than it was back then. You really couldn't have replaced it with anything more the complete opposite of what was there [Eastern Standard]. I guess that's what they were going for.

I think it's like just like punk rock. There's mainstream punk rock— you hear about it in the news and they pretty it up and everything, but there's always gonna be an underground, real punk rock scene. You're always gonna be able to find a scary, shitty bar. You just gotta know where to look.

The Eagle

BOSTON

Anchovies

433 Columbus Ave., Boston
Phone: 617-266-5088

Dive Bar Rating

Dive bars that also pass as Italian restaurants are pretty hard to come by. Like a unicorn in the land of cattle, it's something you're definitely going to remember when you come across one. All the same, people love the food here, pizzas and pastas and comfort food alike. The beer and drinks are on the reasonable side as well, which, considering the neighborhood, anything under $10 is going to be a steal. Just be thankful that somehow a place like this has managed to survive all of these years without being turned into a vegan pet grooming salon and yoga studio.

"It's kind of a nice place in dive bar's clothing," is the way Pat Healy, my editor at the *Metro* newspaper describes it. "Anchovies rules because it's dark as a cave and, no matter how crowded, it isn't a long wait to find a table," says David Day, my editor at the *Weekly Dig*. Who knew it was such a media hangout? "The bar area and its personalities are one thing, but the high-backed booths in the back make you feel like you have the place to yourself."

With apologies to The Eagle, this is *the* South End dive. True to its South End roots it's got a distinctly gay vibe going on in here, although not so much so as the Eagle. It's cramped, cluttered and dark as they come. A jagged little scar of a dive, it's a good antidote to the area's fabulousness.

The bar takes up most of the space in the long, thin room with very low ceilings. Nearly every other inch of space is taken up by random tsotchkes. A stuffed rabbit with antlers oversees the proceedings at the bar. A merry go round horse with a sombrero on keeps him company. Street signs line the walls. Ancient, beat up looking wooden booths seem more like a punishment than a place to relax. Old black and white photos of mustachioed gentlemen and horses pick up the eye candy slack. Overkill? Not really. Here it feels like it's an earned sense of camp. It's a dive, yes. But it's also a "dive." It's a "DIVE!" as well, if that makes any sense.

"Are you gaga for the new disco ball?"

The waitress is talking to the bartender about the room's latest addition.

"Love it!" He says. The crowd coos in excitement when he turns it on. Now we're all bathed in a the rotating glow. A disco ball in a divey, brick wall tavern playing disco pop on the stereo and the football game on TV. Just wow. This place was already teetering on the edge of gay dive insanity. Now the circle is complete. Right now this is a pretty great place to be. Like the best bars, a place like this transforms you to another realm. It transcends its location and time. Outside on the street power couples are power walking their power dogs back to their million dollar brownstone apartments. In here it's just a bar. Not as gritty as some, not as lonely as others, but a dive anyway. Regular people getting drunk, oblivious, at least over the course of a boozy afternoon, and a few revolutions of the disco ball, to the world passing them by outside.

The Bar Room

5 Broad St., Boston
Phone: 617-723-7877

Dive Bar Rating

🍾🍾🍾

As the name would seem to indicate, there isn't too much remarkable about this alley bar hidden in plain view amidst the cavernous high rise corridors of the Financial District. It's just off of the Faneuil Hall area though, so that means you're going to encounter a sunburned Bridge and Tunnel element of twenty and thirty somethings from Revere and Peabody and Saugus and all of the other horrible exurban nightmares of greater-, or lesser rather, Boston. Mostly that's run off from the upstairs night club, which is sort of a vapid, chest and pecs wasteland, although it does host a thriving reggae party. It's the type of club with a mandatory coat check, which is probably functional for some sort of safety reason I guess, but also sounds like a deviant sexual move, or some sort of wrestling grapple hold. The Mandatory Coat Check. Scary.

Where was I? Oh right. The curious thing about this bar is that despite its relative newness—it used to be a place called The Office a couple years ago—it's still a dive. That's something you don't see too often: a brand new dive. Either they planned it that way, or someone spilled a case of Schlitz all over the architect's blueprints. Bars relax into the mold shaped out for them though. So do tits, by the way, of which you'll find a surprising number of the fake sort here. Boston isn't exactly a town known for its plastic surgery demographic, but there's a certain type of townie broad who often works at places like this where they serve a necessary function. Dive tits then, I guess you'd call them.

Speaking of which, I asked the comely lass on duty behind the bar when I came in last what they had in a bottle. "For beer?" Umm... Yes. for beer. I end up with a Magners on the rocks, which is fine since I can pretend to be Irish as well as everyone else around here when I'm drunk. I'm just surprised she didn't call me a fag for ordering it that way.

Down the bar a couple of guys are doing the universally accepted pantomime for doing a bump of coke. That's a pretty good sign that you are not on coke, right? Or does it mean that you really, really are?

Hard to keep track of these things. On the other side of the bar the managers—all burly guys in gold chains with tiny black t-shirts—are pushing chicken parmesan subs into their faces. The rest of the crowd is made up of a few office worker nerds, a handful of biker toughs and their tougher biker girlfriends and exactly two young, cute, confused tourists who I sort of want to rescue like little lost birds and guide them back to the nest.

I'm kind of enamored with the people who work here in all their greasy splendor. It's like watching my own private Massachusetts-based version of the Jersey Shore. That in itself is reason enough to come back here again and again, just to see what drama the next episode is going to offer. Meanwhile the bartenders are dancing. Van Halen is ripping on the juke. A team of dudes are butt-rocking and high-fiving each other in anticipation of all the awesome choices they're going to be making tonight. So we've got bikers, fake tits, Van Halen and coke covered here. Every dive bar is a time machine of some sort, right? This one just doesn't seem to have set its jumping distance back as far as most of the others in this book. That's fine by me. The 1980s needs its dives too.

(Kelsey Marie Bell)

Beacon Hill Pub

148 Charles St., Boston
No phone

Dive Bar Rating

🍾🍾🍾🍾🍾

A dive located on Charles St. is one of those unlikely contradictions that doesn't sound plausible in theory. One of the ritziest streets in the city, it sits at the foot of the old-monied Beacon Hill, home to the State House and the neighborhood that basically invented the idea of the snooty, entitled Boston prick. It's the type of street renowned for its high end antiquing—think about that one for a second—gourmet groceries, art galleries and cute little cafes so precious you could snap them in half with an ill-timed boner. Nearby sailboats glide across the Charles River while sunbathers congregate on the lawns of the Esplanade. Two steps into this bar, which looks like a post apocalyptic bomb shelter on the outside, and all of that melts away.

There's some evidence of money, or power at least, on the inside on busy weekends when young State House staffers still close enough to graduation to feel at home in a dive relax their starched collars to rub up against actual college kids too poor to turn down the cheap beer, or too stupid to know any better. On Fridays and Saturdays the stench of beer and hormones mingle in a potent olfactory cocktail.

The décor is hard to describe. Entropy at work gets close to the mark. Bars like this don't decorate, they accumulate. Like a ball of tape rolling down a hill of dirt, eventually it grabs up a bit of everything. Exposed brick walls covered in years worth of chalk scribblings give way to stained glass windows, a non-functioning fireplace, and the usual random wall hangings. Above the bar you'll find an old acoustically purposed ceiling that's evidence of the spot's history as a piano bar. The high-backed bar chairs are as rickety as some of the patrons availing themselves of low-priced booze earlier in the evening. There are two ladies rooms, which is encouraging, because at least you know that means enough of them come here to necessitate it.

I found a group of old timers talking shit at one end of the bar while a gaggle of Todd and Sarahs hoisted pints of Blue Moon at the other. The beer selection caters to both crowds. Busch Lights are $2.50. A garrulous, homeless sort in a wheel chair buzzed around the room offering to share his chips and salsa with anyone who'd take him up. A thirty something scientist dug in and began explaining the robots his company builds to sell to the military. Who says people in Boston aren't friendly? There's no other food here, but bringing your own is fine. Get a pizza delivered to the door if you like.

"You couldn't open a bar tomorrow that didn't sell food," bartender Kevin explained. "This is one of the last places grandfathered in." It's true. Even at most dives in Boston the arbitrary and ridiculous liquor laws require food to be sold. "We encourage people to order take out," he said. "We have menus behind the bar."

Where there are takeout menus you can usually find college kids. "We have a lot of MIT grad school kids," he said. "A lot of softball teams." So why else do they come? "The booze is cheap." Even better? They're open 365 days of the year. "We're well known for being open every night," he said. That's great for holidays, especially when you need to sneak away from the family for a few hours. Or all night, every night.

Biddy Early's

141 Pearl St., Boston
Phone: 617-654-9944

Dive Bar Rating

A dive bar is a space of illogical juxtapositions; the incongruity of its original décor pushing up against the encroachment of modernity. Which makes sense when you consider that dives themselves are illogical juxtapositions within a contemporary city. So it's not out of the ordinary to find a place like Biddy Early's where two-handed wooden saws and horse cart harnesses hang on the wall above video games and internet jukeboxes. Where delicate China is arranged in shelves by a sign advertising five red headed slut shots for $20. Where old locals drink side by side with Financial District suits loosening the tie for a post work piss up. It's a place for both professionals and for professional drinkers. People who are serious about what they do, even if what they do is mainly drink.

"It's weird man," my friend Nick tells me. He's spent a few dirty evenings here. "I don't think there are any signs outside of it other than 'Saloon.' It's right next to a little lunch-time deli, buried in the Financial District, and the evening crowd is a weird mix of blue collar dudes and professionals. It's definitely dirty, and when young guys bring in dates, the older grizzled dudes will sit down at your table and hit on your lady."

The bar is thriving on a Thursday when we come in. It usually is after work. Even more so during the lunch rush. Liquid lunch is still in the cards for money types and bike messengers, even if it's frowned upon in the real world where most of us live. Kids are shooting darts, and a good part of the crowd is glued to the Bruins playoff game on the tube. Lady Gaga is playing on the stereo—like I said, illogical juxtapositions. It smells like girls in here. Girls and nachos. Two of the best smells I can think of.

A guy at the bar reading the *Herald* is bitching about Sarah Palin. "She's destroying the country!" he says. She was just in town recently with her merry band of tea party idiots descending on the Boston Common not too far from here.

The room is the length of a city block, which is rarer and rarer these days. You could walk in one side, drink your pint along the way and leave without breaking a straight line. It's homey though, after a fashion. A large stone hearth behind the bar and the Irish knick-knacks strewn throughout affect a local pub in the old country feel. The old boxy black telephone behind the bar is out of its time and place. Seems better suited for whacking someone over the head than making an actual call. Half the people in here have probably never even used one of those in their lives. The walls are lined with other curiosities; pots and pans, old photos. In another context it would work toward a rustic charm, here in downtown Boston with a crowd of yuppies in party mode it reminds me more of the time I had a kegger at my grandmother's house in high school while she was away. Everyone was wasted, and nobody appreciated the value of her antiques.

David is drinking with me tonight. He's from outside Dublin, so I press him on the Irish authenticity. The walls of plates stand out for him. "It's like an old Irish thing. On your wedding you'd get a set of China. It's a classic gift. You'd put it on display and use it for Christmas or Easter. Otherwise you wouldn't use it unless the Kennedy's were coming to dinner."

It feels pretty damn far from Easter dinner in here right now. Although it's given me a few ideas. Maybe this year I'll see if I can set up a dart board in the dining room and ask my mom to serve a round of red headed sluts. I can think of weirder juxtapositions.

Black Horse Tavern

340 Fanueil Hall Marketplace, Boston
No Phone

Dive Bar Rating

The Faneuil Hall area is ground zero for tourists in Boston. It also happens to be the center of much of the city's history. Some of the bars in the vicinity like the Bell in Hand Tavern and the Green Dragon date back to Revolutionary times. Not sure what Paul Revere and his drinking buddies might have made of the setting now. Did they have a Gap and a Hard Rock Cafe back then?

Compared to Durgin Park, most of the relatively older bars in this book look a little wet behind the ears. "Established before you were born" boasts the sign on the facade, and unless there's something you aren't telling us, they're right. The communal style seafood and hearty Yankee fair restaurant has been an attraction for locals and tourists alike since 1827, although there have been restaurants in this former Revolutionary era warehouse since 1742. The spot was originally opened to feed the crews of ships docked in the harbor and farmers after a day of selling goods at the nearby Haymarket. There's no bar in the main restaurant area though, so you'll want to head to the basement to check out the Black Horse Tavern. Just like it is now, back in the early 19th century all of the best drinking was done underground.

But for all that history contained in these walls, the Black Horse bar looks more like it was constructed in the 1960s. Cracked vinyl booths along one wall, and kitschy (but unintentionally so) lighting are perversions of the idea of history itself. The floor is brick, which is charming at first, but loses that effect when you try to move your bar stool around at all or take a few errant beer-sodden steps. The space is cramped and haggard in all the right ways if you're looking for a dive though. Whether or not the stench of beer-rot is a hundred years old, or just of last night's vintage is hard to tell.

What can you say, bartender Dave tells me, "The building has been here since 1742. That explains a lot of our leaky plumbing." Dave has only been here a year himself, but he's settled in. I'm literally the only other person in the room when we meet, and it's a spooky scene. Country music blares from a stereo at one end of the bar and Bruce

Willis is kicking someone's ass on an ancient TV on the other. On weekend nights they've got live music. "We have a speaker outside when the band plays and that brings people in," he says. "You only need fifteen people and the place looks full. People like that for some reason."

People also seem to like stapling hand decorated dollar bills to the walls and ceiling above the bar. The place is wall-papered with them. It's like graffiti that costs a buck. "I've had people come back a year later and their dollar is still there," says Dave. "Look, there's a mouse!" he points out. I'm startled for a second. Not because I'm scared of mice, just that I've never seen a bartender go out of his way to point one out. "Did I mention this place is two hundred years old?"

Corner Pub

162 Lincoln St., Boston
Phone: 617-542-7080

Dive Bar Rating

It's eery down here at night. Suspiciously quiet. It's easy to imagine yourself wandering the streets of a post-apocalyptic nightmare if you squint your eyes just so. It's also brutally cold on a February Sunday, and the wind is whipping through the cavern of high rises —nearly all of them lights out by this point, making the long trek from Downtown Crossing all the more intolerable. Unless you're in transit at nearby South Station, or one of those unfortunate souls who spend their days at, god forbid, an actual office job in the nearby Financial District, there really isn't any other reason to be on this block anyway. Chinatown is just over yonder, and it's brimming with life as usual. The lights are glowing over the iconic arch as I round the corner onto Lincoln Street.

The siren-song of Weggies is calling to me. Or is it the swan song? The beloved Boston dive institution is long gone by now. In all of the discussions about dives I've been having with people over the past year it's one of the most lamented bar losses that comes up time and time again. They've remodeled in here, and changed the name, but that turned out to be mostly wishful thinking on the owners part.

Back then it was a popular mid-afternoon stop-off for droves of Big Dig workers looking to wind down or charge up before and after a long day of driving a tunnel through the heart of the city. Perhaps they gang-pressed one or two of them with lengthy bar tabs to throw in some work on the bar, because it's a pretty decent looking transformation they've done in here. The brick facade and iron bars on the windows are still as imposing as ever though.

"We essentially gutted the entire place," says owner Matt Chin. "The most noticeable changes (for customers) would be the reconfiguration and new bar. The bathrooms were renovated and repositioned. The kitchen was updated—yes, there was a kitchen at Weggies."

"Our biggest concern was renovating it so we were able to keep the true regulars returning, but cleaning it up enough for new clientele to start coming in. The one thing we don't get hardly at all anymore is people coming in and trying to buy their $3 beer with change. I actually was the on-call bartender for Weggies starting in 1995, so it's been really great to see that part of the 'customer base' move on."

Tonight the customer base includes myself, the bartender, and three or four old Chinese men drinking quietly and watching the Pro Bowl. That's one of the other cool things about this spot. Unlike almost every other dive bar in Boston, it's got a strong Asian feel here. Obviously the proximity to Chinatown has a lot to do with that. "Tipping is not a city in China" is a sign you'll see at a lot of dives. Not many of them in Boston have a group of regulars who might know from first hand experience.

Talk at the bar turns to football. Everyone's a big Patriots fan, no surprise, but Peyton Manning is just better right now, they all agree. Some dive discussions are universal. I'm a little reluctant to open my yap, since unlike most of these guys these bar stools don't seem to have memorized the contours of my ass cheeks, but then talk turns to the spread on the game and now we're all friends. One of the guys has a little action on the game. "Hey, it's the Pro Bowl, you don't have to try so hard!" he shouts. It's the same thing here. In fact you don't really have to try at all.

Delux Cafe

100 Chandler St., Boston
Phone: 617-338-5258

Dive Bar Rating

It'd be easy to overlook this hidden favorite if you were walking down Chandler St. from the Back Bay to the South End. A corner bar with no windows and a discreet door, it's a room that invests patrons with a sense of accomplishment for finding it. But make no mistake, plenty of people do find it. When asking around about favorite dives in Boston, Delux came up time and time again. That's partly because it's a longstanding neighborhood classic, but also because it falls squarely on the hipster side of the dive bar line of demarcation. The cute young tattooed servers and bartenders, and a bespectacled clientele here are all reaching for an air of authenticity in a decidedly overly stylized part of the city. For the most part they've found it.

It's not your father's dive by any stretch. The relatively quality comfort food offerings, and busy dinner time crowd here see to that. Bottles of Sriracha on the table are a pretty good giveaway about the people who eat here. Hipsters love their ethnic hot sauce don't they?

Nonetheless it's scuzzy enough to qualify, albeit as more of a rock and roll dive than an old local's watering hole. And considering its locale, it's on the cheap side as well.

Amanda Palmer of the Dresden Dolls lives nearby, and it's a bar she recommended when I cornered her for an opinion on the dives of Boston.

"It's one of my favorite places, and you could certainly classify it as a dive in that it's a place that you can get liquor and food without feeling like you've been financially raped. It's got a funk. It's exactly my style. Places like that that are covered from floor to ceiling with visual explosion I feel right at home at."

Marlon Brando jockeys for space with Mickey Mouse and a statue of Narcissus. A bust of Elvis in the corner sits along with a stuffed rabbit head with antlers. The graffiti-ravaged bathrooms too are an object lesson in sensory overkill. They're somewhere between an untalented tagger and a prolific serial killer's idea of how to decorate a dungeon wall.

It's the bar room walls papered with LP record sleeves that really

Delux Cafe

tie the room—and the overall aesthetic of the bar and its patrons—together however. The Sex Pistols, The Clash and The Monkees and everything in between. They're all closer together than you'd think in a place like this where the music becomes the vibe, genres blend, retroism rules and old is new. Social Distortion and Sinatra volley back and forth on the soundtrack here, and somewhere in that vast space is encapsulated the worldview of the type of throwback hipster who calls the Delux home. If you condensed that stereotypical drinker's beer-infused blood into solid form, built a bar with it, then let an army of well-heeled heathens in lower-class drag roll it in the dirt, the Delux is what you'd end up with.

(Kelsey Marie Bell)

BOSTON

BOSTON'S BEST DIVE BARS

The Dugout

722 Commonwealth Ave., Boston
Phone: 215-339-9282

Boston University students are a pretty convenient scapegoat for whatever problem an old city grump wants to complain about today. They make the bars overcrowded. They turn the Green Line into a house party on weekend nights with their drunk-in-public obliviousness. The relentless onslaught of their school's real estate grab has homogenized entire chunks of the city, particularly gritty old Kenmore Square. They've turned many great old bars into shit shows with their damned youthful fun-having! And just try driving down Comm. Ave when school is in session. This is a busy city artery, kids. If you're gonna cross in packs against the light at least walk faster.

I'm having flashbacks to college myself when I walk into The Dugout. How much are they gonna charge for a keg cup here? Will the girl from 18th Century English poetry be here? That's mostly because the lay out of this basement bar brings to mind some crusty old frat house. It smells like beer, and it looks like beer, if that makes any sense. The lounge room area in back has bro man dude written all over it as well. Slumpy couches, mismatched lamps, dart board. In short, it's a classic college dive.

Or is it?

"That's probably how we'd classify ourselves, gun to the head," bartender Dave tells me. He's been here for five years. Although he spent his college days at Tufts at the divey Sligo, he says.

The history of the bar goes back a lot further though. And what a history it is. Open since 1934, a plaque in the back room tells the story of its original owner, Jimmy O'Keefe, a veritable Boston legend. It talks about how O'Keefe helped elect Boston Mayor then Governor Maurice Tobin. Apparently after Tobin didn't come through on a promise to get a man who'd held signs for him in the campaign a job, O'Keefe beat his ass. He beat up the governor. Think about that. O'Keefe was also a bootlegger in the thirties, and Ted Williams used to drive his car. Total. Bad. Ass.

Today it's not quite so monumental in here. It's changed over the years, although not so much that a guy who came in the other day who used to go to school at BU in the sixties was remarking to Dave about how much things have stayed the same. "This place spans generations for the BU crowd," he tells me.

Dave seems a little conflicted about the dive moniker though. He explains. "The problem is people equate dives with shit holes. Just because you're a dive doesn't mean you're not clean, or you're not safe. It's just not $12 martinis, a door guy out front with an ear piece and a velvet rope." It helps if you have a popcorn machine on the bar, $3 PBRs, a cash only sign and an old school register I tell him.

The no violence thing though? That's something I can get behind.

"I've never seen anything close to a fight. It's not a high intensity bar. Mainly grad students, professors and their TAs and university maintenance guys who finished their shift having a couple of Buds. It's fun because the bar is set up so they all get to know each other because it's L-shaped." I just wish O'Keefe was still around to meet at the bar. Now there's a guy I'd like to get to know.

The Eagle

520 Tremont St., Boston
Phone: 617-542-4494

Dive Bar Rating

Since the mid nineteenth century, when many of the five story redbrick row houses that line the streets of the South End were being built, this has been a neighborhood in flux. As the twentieth century dawned, and newer neighborhoods like the Back Bay became more fashionable, the South End began to be populated by middle-class black families and large numbers of immigrants, a sense of relative diversity that persists to this day despite the area's recent development into one of the more fashionable restaurant and art districts in the city. There were long stretches of time however, where the South End was a troubled neighborhood, and for many, an undesirable place to live. After World War II, as is always the case, fringe populations like artists, gays and lesbians and bohemians recognized the South End's potential and began what has become by now a familiar process of rejuvenation: marginalized progressive groups move in, fashionable middle class soon follow, and eventually property values are driven up so high that no one but the wealthy can live there.

I mention that in respect to the Eagle, because as one of Boston's last remaining true gay bars, and one of the only gay dives at all, its three decades at the center of this politically, and fashionably charged area is remarkable, and the trends one traces through the history of gay bars in Boston are relevant to the ways dive bars have been elbowed aside over the years for higher end, more "respectable" businesses. In the 1990s there were about 16 gay bars in Boston. Now there are roughly 7. Dive bars like the ones covered in this book have faired even worse. The whitewashing of neighborhoods like the South End is part of a much larger trend sweeping throughout cities like Boston in general. First the gay bars, then the dive bars are dislocated. Then the independent book stores and marginal ethnic restaurants and other speciality shops go next.

Roger has been bartending at The Eagle through much of that evolution. He's been here since 1981 when they opened their doors.

"This area was so gay in the seventies and eighties," he says. "Back then you would see a lot of guys walking down the streets holding hands. Now all you see is baby strollers and yuppies." This was a very skeevy area back then, he says. "No one wanted to come here except the gays, who came because it was so cheap.

Today the Eagle, unlike many of the gay bars throughout the country that share the name, isn't much of a leather bar. But it's still a notorious spot for cruising, particularly late at night. "The Eagle is called the Dirty Bird and is frequently seen as the last chance hook up bar at 1:30. It is a meat market and at 2 you will see the best sidewalk sale in Boston," says Kelly, a sommelier at a decidedly non-divey restaurant nearby. Michael Brodeur, my editor at the *Boston Globe* says it's a poor example of the Eagle name. "Unfriendly barkeep, stale atmosphere, bad music. So sad, but she has to want to help herself to get better."

I found the room welcoming, if dingy and a bit downtrodden. Good dive qualities. Roger was extraordinarily helpful and friendly. The high tin ceilings are littered with all manner of flags and banners —sports teams, country flags, gay men's clubs' colors—and the walls are covered with wooden eagle statues and stuffed animal heads. It looks like the type of haunted house theme park attraction where you'd expect everything to spring to life like clockwork and scare the shit out of you.

Back when he first lived in the neighborhood you could rent an apartment nearby on the cheap, Roger says. He lived upstairs from the bar for sixteen years. "That's how bad the neighborhood was, you couldn't even rent these beautiful apartments." Doesn't seem to be a problem renting them anymore. It's just a different class of people now. That's a little scary too.

Interview with Amanda Palmer of the Dresden Dolls

Amanda Palmer is one of the best examples of a rock star we've got living in the city right now. I asked her about what makes a dive a dive, and some of her favorites in the city.

What are some of your favorite dive bars in Boston?

How broadly are you classifying dive bars? Depending on how you're defining it there are a couple of places that come to mind. One that I consider that was the most obvious was the Abbey Lounge. It was awesome in its unabashed embrace of its own diveyness, which is odd for Boston, because it usually isn't very meta about life. I loved the fact that the Abbey was like the dive bar with the website that tooted its own horn about how divey it was. Kind of made you love it.

Right, it was kind of a dive website. What about places that are still around?

One of my favorite places, you could certainly classify it as a dive in that it's a place that you can get liquor and food without feeling like you've been financially raped, is Deluxe which is not far from where I live in the South End. It's not the Franklin Cafe, and it's got a funk, without over-charging you for stuff. It's exactly my style, places like that that are covered from floor to ceiling with visual explosion I feel right at home. I'm a pack rat and I love constant stimulation. I remember sitting there and really studying the record album covers they have on the walls. That's the type of thing that can feel educational, you go in there and you're getting an education on sixties albums covers. I'm a dorky musician but that turns me on.

You don't normally think of dives when you think of the South End, but there are a few holdouts. Like Wally's.

I'm touring all the time so I'm not always going to these places, but Wally's definitely doesn't change much. Most people who aren't in the neighborhood or Berklee types wouldn't deliberately head there.

But that place is a joint. It's a serious joint. The most interesting thing about that place is you get this weird fucked up combination of students and black people from the neighborhood who have nothing in common, but they both wind up there. Depending on the night it can feel like one or the other of those groups are acting like tourists and the other are acting like regulars. You get full on dive joint treatment when you go there. I love that.

Do you find the dives in Boston to be different than the ones you see on tour?

Every city has its own bar culture. Boston's bar culture from place to place is kind of unique. I used to live in Germany and there is like the universal way that a bar would present itself from the outside to say "this is a local bar for old guys you don't come in here if you're looking to have a beer with your friends, and we are going to indicate this by this, this and this." There's a way a bar in Boston presents itself from the outside that invites or disinvites people and it has to do with beer signs and Keno signs or this that and the other thing. But it's funny because hipsters are weird because they can adopt a dive bar for a while. It's funny to watch the collision of the crusty old guys sitting at the bar and the hipsters ordering PBR deciding this is their new bar.

I have a hard time finding bars I like. You think for a city this size with this many students and this many people and different kinds of people there would be some places that would be funkier. I feel like it's a choice between all these chichi places with people I have nothing in common with and I feel like an alien or it's...I don't even know. I go to other cities and their bars are more friendlier. I think the Middle East is the closest thing that everybody knows where the young people come out.

JJ Donovan's

27 Clinton St., Boston
Phone: 617-523-9522

Dive Bar Rating

Irish pubs are a dime a dozen in Boston. Irish dives that have been owned continuously by the same family for almost two hundred years? Not so much. Save this one, opened in the early nineteenth century. It's in the same old warehouse building that houses the ancient Durgin Park, although its affect is a little less historically inclined. A small, squat, brightly lit room comprised almost entirely of the u-shaped bar, it's extraordinarily uncluttered, like a minimalist theater director's deconstruction of a dive.

It's peculiarly bright in here as well. There are so many beer signs and the overhead lights are on such a full blast, it's like drinking on the surface of the sun. Curious contradiction you'll find in your dive-going treks. They'll either be sarcophagi of damp shame or blazing with fluorescent heat.

Outside a bespectacled grad-school type is complaining to his cute Asian girlfriend that everyone is looking at him. It only took me about five seconds into my beer to understand how he felt. A young Bob Hoskins is drinking a pint menacingly next to a scrum of rugby sized boozers. A woozy Barney Frank lookalike in a Sox cap has definitely got a looking problem. The lads are pumping dollars into the jukebox, keeping the room buzzing with a steady procession of The Clash and Oasis. This is still touristy Faneuil Hall though, right? How'd I find myself cast in the middle of a Guy Ritchie film? I'm playing the role of sniveling mark in this one. The bartender is pleasant though, offering up a styrofoam plate of chips and pretzels for me to snack on. And snack I do, like that plate was a lifeline to shore. "We've been opened since 1826," he said. "We rent the upstairs floor to Durgin Park. That's how we're able to keep it kind of cool in here and not as touristy."

Not a tourist in sight now, unless you count me. At least the shit-faced Latino next to me, all bleary-eyed and jittery must feel even more out of place. Wait a second, here's the owner coming over to wish him a happy birthday. You know what they say about a poker table? If you've been sitting there for a while trying to figure out who the asshole is for too long it's probably you.

JJ Foley's

21 Kingston St., Boston
Phone: 617-695-2529

Dive Bar Rating

Some dives feel like they've always been holes in the wall. Others, with a more lengthy run like this one—the original Foley's on East Berkeley opened in 1909, this second location a few decades later in 1959—are charged with an age old grandeur. The shine may be off the gem so to speak, but the room still reverberates with echoes of history.

The original locale has gone soft on us with its newish Irish pub sheen. The halfway house is still next door, but there's also a yoga studio nearby. Kingston Street hasn't changed enough to escape its essence though. Boston drinkers of all stripes have lent their livers to the cause here over the years. The most notable story people like to tell is the time Bono showed up after a gig at the Garden. Joe Strummer drank here too. I'd probably still be telling that story myself if I was there. Although newcomers to the bar may be surprised to get anything in the way of talk from the curt barmen, all attired in crisp white shirts, suspenders and been there done that indifference.

Back before the smoking ban the large back dining room here was a great place to catch a mid-workday case of second hand lung cancer. Before that it was known to stay open way past closing hour thanks to the type of influential patrons the bar has long served. Or so the rumors have it. Today you won't see as many pols or newsmen as you might have taking in a wet lunch, and the hipster quotient has died down a bit as well. For years this was known as the spot for bike messengers and their similarly dirty, tattooed brethren to fuel up between jaunts. I should know. In the early 2000s when the *Weekly Dig* offices were located in a cramped loft just up the street this was our regular.

It's not hard to see why all the varied walks of Boston booze life would find comfort here. It's a large, stately beer hall with high ceilings, dark stained wooden fixtures, and an old country air, not to mention a miserably shitty men's room that feel likes a graffiti-strewn coffin. It feels like a good spot for a rousing sing-song, a political meeting or a post-donnybrook pint. Maybe all three.

The Penalty Box

65 Causeway St., Boston
No Phone

It's been about five or six years since I've been into the Penalty Box, and a lot has changed. No, not about the bar. Like any dive worth its sketchy tap lines the room hasn't undergone anything in the way of improvements. Mostly it's the neighborhood outside. A massive construction project that transferred the T underground has completely opened up the area of Causeway St. around the Boston Garden. The tracks used to hang over the street like a wet, dismal canopy, blotting out the sun like the sort of dismal, shadowy overpass on which you might expect to find a vigilant Batman surveying the miscreants below.

Another thing that's changed is that there doesn't happen to be a long line of mods and anglophile hipsters queued up inside waiting to get upstairs only to find themselves banished to this divey purgatory when they arrived too-fashionably late. For years the long-running Brit indie dance party The Pill threw down in the venue upstairs here. The Pill moved across town to the slightly less divey Great Scott in Allston a ways back, and when I stop in here the place has been completely scrubbed clean of its stylish ghost. I spent so much time here in my early twenties that in a way it was like being the only person to show up for my college reunion. The contrast of the fancy boys who like girls who like boys like their girls and the grizzled veterans who spent their night propped up here was captivating cultural contrast. Now there's a thick-necked cop type eating take out on the bar, and a brassy old broad in a Bruins sweater slinging Bud to a thin crowd. A woman my grandmother's age is putting the moves on a Dave Chapelle caricature way too young for her daughter, but he's rolling with it. At a place like this age doesn't really exist.

Turns out that after the tragic fires at the Station nightclub in Rhode Island fire inspectors got all up in everyone's shit, the manager explains when I asked about the lack of entertainment upstairs anymore. Stricter regulations forced them to shut down. "They've had a hard-on for this place for a while," he says.

The beer is still cold though, and the atmosphere is still "real,"

BOSTON'S BEST DIVE BARS

whatever that's worth. Decorative sports and beer banner flags dangle from the drop tile ceilings in the type of cluelessly decorative touch that is almost heartbreaking in its ineffectiveness. The framed pictures of old boxers and the historically decadent Scollay Square neighborhood of Boston add a touch of nostalgia. It's comforting that at least someone around here remembers the old days. Out of nowhere a Garbage song comes on the shitty stereo behind the bar drowning out the sound of the local news broadcast on the boxy old TVs propped here and there. Grandma tries out a few grinding moves while a dude in a non-ironic trucker cap is getting shut off at the bar. For the first time in a while I actually feel a little nervous sitting with my back to the door in a bar. The Penalty Box name suddenly seems apt. What did I do to get sentenced here?

"I wish we still had stuff going on upstairs," the manager says. "I had a ball up there." I did too.

Punter's Pub

450 Huntington Ave., Boston
Phone:617-472-2330

Dive Bar Rating

This corner bar on busy Huntington takes the triangle shape of the streets it abuts, expanding outward from a point to a wide game room adjacent to a pizza shop where you can order pies through a hole in the wall. The turd-brown wooden slats of the exterior would make the bar standout anyway, but its location directly across the street from the Museum of Fine Arts presents a striking contrast. You could spend decades of your life drinking in this bar without ever crossing over the tracks, literal and metaphoric, that separate it from the museum.

The rustic wooden theme carries over to the interior of the bar as well. Its beat up wooden brown on the walls, the booths and the bar. You need a sturdy, forgiving design to deal with the influx of frat dudes and Northeastern athletes for whom this bar has served as a clubhouse since it opened in 1970. The rows and rows of framed and signed team photos on the walls attest to that.

"It's a big college bar, especially when Northeastern and Wentworth are in," the bartender says. "Big time." My friend Rebecca was one of those students not long ago. "The crowd was always pretty much wrecked," she says. Lindsay, who just graduated from NU, says she barely remembers most of her nights here. "Punter's was literally a place to get wasted, nothing else. A total dump. It's mostly men at Punter's, or the sluts who were looking to get laid by the football players." Indeed.

There are a few athletes and a smattering of "sluts" drinking pitchers of beer at the bar at the moment, but in an hour it will be heaving in here. Still, with only about twenty drinkers it's stifling. We're in the middle of a ghastly heat wave in Boston, and bars like this don't tend to spring for central air.

They get a lot of construction workers in here in the day time too, the bartender says. A lot of them around with all the new highrises going up.

As we're talking, packs of cute girls in swishing sundresses and their bearded boyfriends are piling in. They're toughing it out despite the heat, soaking up the beer, not sweating nearly as much as I am. I used to be able to do that.

Red Hat Cafe

9 Bowdoin St., Boston
Phone: 215-467-1752

Dive Bar Rating

The Government Center area is a ghastly wasteland of nothingness. Yes, there are dozens of bars and restaurants to choose from, it's just that, to mangle Gertude Stein, there's no there there. Most of the bars here are after work spots where people who hate their corporate jobs come to dull the monotony of staring into the void.

A steady supply of kids from nearby Suffolk University here at least introduces the possibility of hope. For years the Red Hat was supposed to have been pretty lax when it came to checking IDs. Not any more. Most dives depend on either the really, really old, or the really, really young for business. The balance tips toward the latter here, and toward the female side. It's something like the pink Red Sox hat of dive bars. Perhaps that's who the $2 jello shots advertised on the bar are for? Or the $3 Red Hat Punch? "It's a bunch of stuff with pineapple juice," bartender Danielle tells me, which somehow, against all odds, sounds just mysterious enough to order.

Female clientele notwithstanding, if your interior décor incorporates dangling white christmas lights and stacks of empty beer cases into its scheme somehow, you are a dive. I'm sorry, I don't care how many fresh-faced Econ majors stop by to eat chicken sandwiches and finger bang the touch screen video game screen. You'll find one of those, as well as a popcorn machine and the requisite jukebox, in the basement level bar. There's something about drinking underground that's so primal. It's like cavemen gathered around a fire, or a keg of Miller High Life. Either one really.

"We opened over 100 years ago catering to sailors, dockworkers an ship builders," Danielle tells me. The Red Hat stayed open as a speakeasy throughout Prohibition.

Coincidentally, the girl seated next to me at the bar stopped in because her grandfather used to own a speakeasy in the area. She thought this might be the one.

"It's too bright in here," she says. Is it divey enough though? "I don't know what makes a dive bar a dive bar," she said. "It has to smell like stale beer. It's got to be like when you're waking up the next morning after hosting a party." Close enough.

Remmingtons

124 Boylston St, Boston
Phone: 617-574-9676

Dive Bar Rating

Opened since 1984, this restaurant and bar housed in a former bank has somehow managed to fight off the beautification of both the block in general and the people who hang out here. At night the well- and high-heeled party set line up around the corner in the Alley and at the neighboring Gypsy Bar, two of the "hottest" nightclub areas in the city. On the one hand you're happy to see this throwback maintain its sense of style in the face of the swanky ultra-lounge douche onslaught, but on the other you wonder if they haven't learned any lessons at all on making money from their handsome, busier neighbors.

It's also located directly across the street from a cemetery on the Boston Common, which makes sense, because this place has the grim look of death about it. Surprisingly that makes it a great spot for a comedy club too. Most nights of the week the downstairs room (complete with the bank's original vault) turns into a comedy club that's a regular stop on the circuit for local talent on the way up (and down).

The main room of the bar pays homage to the Theatre District neighborhood's show-biz shine with autographed cast posters from productions like *The Producers* and *Phantom of the Opera*. At the bar itself a cast of characters looks like they could be the understudies for feature roles as dive bar cliches. Don't be surprised to find yourself squeezing into a seat at the bar between a hopped up comedian on one end yapping into the blower about his set tonight and a stone-grilled old timer scowling into his whiskey and worrying over a Keno ticket. Otherwise you might find side-burned bro-hammers scarfing down cheap pizza and beer pitcher specials, or theatre-going families not exactly excited about the scene, but happy to be eating on the cheap after whatever price-gouging musical they just escaped from.

The waitresses are a mix of tragic creative types from nearby Emerson suffering from bouts of weltschmerz and older broads too seasoned to give a shit about sitting down on the job during a slow stretch. The TVs are old, but the Keno and horse racing screens aren't, and there's a scratch ticket machine at the end of the bar, so unlike nearly every bar in Boston the Red Sox seem to take a backseat to the numbers here. There's also one of those old candy machines with a pile of year old m+ms for a quarter. After a Sam Adams or two I wasn't too shy to try it out. Surprisingly acceptable grub, and the shit-eating grin of the friendly—but not too friendly—bartender make this a place I find myself more often than I'd expect.

Shangrilla Chinese Restaurant

138 Cambridge St, Boston
Phone: 617-523-0557

Dive Bar Rating

When this restaurant opened forty years ago, the tiki lounge aesthetic of the tiny bar room in the back was on the cutting edge. Chinese restaurants did a lot to popularize the idea of lounges in general in American cities. In fact growing up in the suburbs of Boston I remember that in most towns the only options for a bar where you could get a mixed cocktail and sit in vinyl booths in low lit rooms were in Chinese joints.

For better or worse the room as you see it today is pretty much exactly as it was when it was built. One wall is covered in a dusty looking mirror that somehow makes the space feel smaller as opposed to opening it up. It's like drinking in a cramped utility shed. There are low marble tables surrounded by mismatched hotel meeting room chairs. The dark flowered wall paper sags off the walls in long curling leaves, maybe the product of the two space heaters rotating in the corners. Sitting at the bar you're met with alternative currents of dry, scorching heat and bracing cold. Maybe that's where the smell of wet dog comes from as well. After a few drinks I could feel the must seeping into my bones. I started to question whether or not it was me or the bar itself.

For now it's just me, my friend David and one other drinker at the bar. We order two Manhattans, but watching the old Chinese bartender prepare them, David thinks better of it and switches to a bottled beer. The bartender moves at the speed of viscous crab rangoon sliding off the side of a table. I stick it out. It's actually pretty good. An ancient white guy in a track suit is watching "Law and Order" on the old TV. "Prostitution!" he yells. "No one can lie better than a good hooker." I have to take his word on that one.

There are scorpion bowls stacked high on the back of the bar. They get a lot more work later at night when the Emerson and Suffolk kids slop through on their bar crawls. For years this has been a popular spot for college kids looking to sneak a few underage cocktails in. The cheap scorpion bowls are part of the appeal. You won't catch them here unless they're shit faced though. At one point a group of four young girls wander into the bar, stand by the door and immediately turn around and leave in horror. God, the look on their face. I feel like I now know what it's like to be the disappointing ugly guy on a blind date.

The restaurant side of the building is apparently reasonably popular, but it's no less improved upon. It has the stark, barely maintained feel of a sketchy front operation. Downstairs on the way to the bathroom there is a hallway with a half dozen unmarked doorways that seem like they could literally lead anywhere. It's like that scene in the *Matrix* where each door leads to another part of the world. I wouldn't have been surprised to open one of them and find a Tibetan mountain temple. The doors I tried were all locked though. Come to think of it, probably better off for me that they were.

"It's like retro loungey in here, but it looks like they got lost somewhere along the way," David tells me. He's slathering red chillies onto fried shrimp at the bar. There's a cracked vinyl booth in the corner. The beer lights hanging from the ceiling are so old they don't even glow anymore. "You see places like this sprout up all the time now," he says. This is like the new lounge model, except, you know, minus the new part. Also the ability to actually lounge part.

"It's just so baffling to me that a place like this still exists," I tell him. "In this Beacon Hill locale."

"It hasn't changed in forty years," the bar man tells me. I'm about to ask him more but a gay man and his middle aged beard wander in and orders mai tais. They're regulars and they're arguing with the other drinker at the bar about what to watch on TV next. *Survivor* is coming on soon apparently. Considering this bar, that's an apt choice.

Interview with Zane Lamprey

Zane Lamprey is an asshole. No, not because of anything he did. It's just that the comedian invented the type of dream job that literally every single person reading this wishes they had before any of us could think of it first. With his shows like *Three Sheets* and *Drinking Made Easy* he travels around the world sampling locally produced alcohol and immersing himself in each country's drinking customs.

What is a dive bar exactly?

Why do we choose a bar to go to? Let's say someone who maybe doesn't drink for a living, they're home, they're gonna call their buddy "Hey, let's go out, grab a drink." Where are they gonna go? There's a number of factors involved there. Members of the opposite sex, which is what they're looking for, the vibe of the place, the music. But ultimately it's the people that they're going to interact with when they get there. A dive bar is probably a bar that's been around for a while, and people love it. The thing is with dive bars, they typically realize that it's the people that make the place, so then they say "Forget about the décor, we don't care, it's about the people that are there." They don't care about what's on the walls, they care about what's inside those four walls. But I don't know what defines a dive bar. I would say 50% of dives bar would say they're not dive bars.

How do you know when you've wandered in a dive bar where you probably don't belong.

I don't want a place where people are bringing their problems. I don't need a place where I have to worry about my safety. We've had a few situations over the last five years shooting where we walk in and the locals don't want us there. You don't want me there, I don't want to be there. You want to be some place where you're wanted. That's basically the only time I wouldn't want to be some place. If some places is super cheesey, or has a theme, sometimes that kind of stuff is fun, but it just comes down to the people.

There are places that become adopted by twenty something kids that are shit holes, then the place next door can be empty with two old dudes. What's that all about?

It's a cliché, but people go where people go. We have a hot dog stand in LA called Pigs and there's always a line for the hot dogs. Any time of day there is always a line. And I don't think anybody knows why. They aren't the planet's best hot dogs. There's not like something magic inside them. It's just people go where people go because people go there. I don't know. I think it takes some sort of enigmatic personality that starts the trend, then you have a few more big personalities that adopt it, and there you go, now you've got a place. Until those people decide they're not going to go there anymore and the trend starts to go away. Same thing, it comes down to the people. It's not about what they're serving, it's about the people that are there.

Sidebar

14 Bromfield St., Boston
Phone: 617-357-1899

Dive Bar Rating

This area of Downtown Crossing has been a bar destination for quite some time. Almost 130 years in fact, if you consider the Marliave, one of the oldest restaurants in the city. Not all of the neighborhood bars have been so fortunate. A few years back the beloved Littlest Bar ended its sixty plus year reign on Province St. as a staple of Boston culture both high and low. It was a spot for politicians from the nearby State House, newly arrived immigrants and shady lowlifes alike. Sidebar hasn't had as illustrious a run as either of those, but on this cavernous old Boston block the streets are paved with history, and any bar down here is going to reflect that in its peculiar design of necessity. This room was probably the height of classy architecture and design a hundred years ago. A bar settles into that skin, like water expanding to fill whatever space you hold it in. Now it's just a cramped first floor dive with odd corners, and a rickety charm catering to twenty something office workers and Suffolk Law students. They're here for the cheap drafts and cheap buffalo wings and to drink out of those tall super pitcher things that look like over-sized beer bongs with a tap. Someone drained his a little too fast tonight actually, because the bathroom is caked in puke. It's 7 p.m. on a Wednesday by the way. Just saying.

By chance I bump into Scott, an old friend from Emerson, when I return from the puke coffin. We used to have fiction writing classes together, which basically means we've got a lot of material to make fun of each other about. "Sidebar is a dive, but more of a fratty dive," he explains draining the last of a Bud Light. "It's almost more of a Suffolk Law douche kind of dive. I swear law school students are almost worse than frat guys. But the bar has its share of rugged, lonely and sometimes weird regulars, who often go solo."

So why does he come back all the time? "You can't beat the price for this part of town," he says. "$2 drafts, $7 pitchers. Some of the bartenders are really nice. One often refuses to take my money and has even forced me to take back a tip. Maybe she appreciates the fact that I'm not a law school student or a rocked, racist, sexist, alcoholic

Vietnam vet?"

Two sides of the customers here summed up in a few words. Maybe those writing classes paid off after all. There are two sides to the space here as well (that's called a transition). We're on the proper bar side. The other is more of a floppy college living room scenario. The dude next to us is plowing through a plate of buffalo wings face first. The smell is so strong I might as well be eating them myself, he's giving me a serious case of bleu cheese nose. On the other side the boys are wilding out in khakis and fleece jackets swaying to Wu Tang. Bros for life. You're my boy man. Pass the beer tower. Actually, don't. I'm gonna puke.

Sullivan's Tap

168 Canal St., Boston
Phone: 617-720-4455

Dive Bar Rating

Located on the type of wind swept urban side street that could either be your idea of the pinnacle of clandestine nightlife or a really good place to get stabbed depending on your outlook, Sully's is the boozy, beating heart of Bruins and Celtics territory. It has been since it opened in 1933, the year after prohibition ended. The corporatization of sporting events in recent years has of course mellowed out the area, but beer and hockey, and the men who love beer and hockey, will never be entirely tamed.

Much of the crowd was lumbering across Causeway St. for the game by the time I rolled in, but moments ago it was thick on the ground with hockey sweaters and goatees. The staff had the shell-shocked look of a band of soldiers that had just survived a night taking heavy fire, although the room is so long – it stretches across a full block between Canal and Friend Streets – one wonders if a door man on one end went down how long it would actually be before his comrades on the other side even noticed. A sign on the wall boasts that it's the longest bar in Boston, and that sounds believable to me.

Speaking of signs, even by dive standards the walls here are plastered with beer specials and sports commemorations. "Watch every game here," reads one. "Watch your belongings," reads another. Good advice. The stacked rows of neon beer signs make this place glow and hum like a beery arcade, and that's before you even consider the actual video game area. Wobbly diner style bar stools and a vaguely sticky, and sticker-covered, bar will be familiar sites and feels to any dive connoisseur. Bright yellow painted squares on the floor however, are a unique touch. They're either shout outs to the Bruins, or more likely, warnings for woozy homers who trip walking up and down the single step to the pool tables. It's cash only here, of course, but there is an ATM that may well be the original prototype machine it seems so old. For a minute I thought maybe I could boot up some old ColecoVision games on that piece. The men's can is a vertigo inducing pattern of black and white tiles. Looks like the type of spot Willy Wonka would go to hurl after thirteen Molson's or to start a beef with a lost Canadiens fan. Good luck finding any privacy in here for that matter. There's no door on the shitter, which is pretty much universal dive speak for "we're sick of dudes blasting rails in here."

Down the bar a group of buddies are talking out loud to no one in particular about how they had tickets for the game they were watching on TV that was taking place literally a few hundred yards away. "I just want to walk into the game for a few minutes so I can say I went," one of the dudes, probably named Steve-O, said. He's got a point. By the same token you'll just have to walk into Sullivan's Tap for a few minutes to say you know what a quintessential dive in Boston is like.

The Tam

222 Tremont St., Boston
No phone

Dive Bar Rating

The Tam is a pretty good illustration of the ways that perspective can change the character of a bar. The angle that you approach it will have a huge effect on your impression. A few blocks away on one side sits the (relatively) beautiful urban pastoral of the Boston Common, million dollar hi-rise condos along the park and the artsy Emerson College where the city's future freelance writers and radio types major in coke and eyeliner. But its locale at the crossroads of Tremont and Kneeland Streets also puts The Tam in the shadow, literally and figuratively, of Boston's notorious Combat Zone. That designation doesn't really exist anymore, as the crime, drugs and prostitution the area was long known for have mostly migrated elsewhere, but that shady trifecta still rears its head from time to time and you'd be naïve to mistake the adjacent blocks east and south of here as completely whitewashed.

That said, despite the influx of Emerson kids and the subsequent "improvements" that come with a younger, monied crowd, the Tam has still retained much of its seedy character, if not exactly the seedy characters themselves from its near fifty years in business. "What you get is what you see" reads the sign behind the bar, and I don't really have any idea what that means, but it sounds exactly right. Inside the bar is home to the usual disastrous interior design decisions that make the best dives what they are. It's so cluttered with decades of accumulated arcana hanging from the ceilings, tucked into corners and peeling off the walls you might feel like you've wandered into the rec room of a time-traveling alcoholic wizard who also happens to be a total Boston sports homer. High def TVs and those odd Barcast advertisement/texting prompt screens seem anachronistic. It's like stopping by grandad's and finding out he's got a newer model iPhone than you.

The Saturday afternoon I stopped in a post-college crowd were watching a couple football games while the young, mustachioed (irony status inconclusive) bartender mixed me a Manhattan with aplomb and courtesy. More cute girls in attendance than you might expect, but they were balanced out by what you might call the Boston dude: a pale, wobbly Michael Rappaport character with a Celtics jersey on only two shots shy of getting retarded in some kid's face.

A duo of tourists from Buffalo or Canada (same thing) wandered in to use the ladies room, which apparently is kept locked at all hours. What's that all about? "When I first got here I wondered the same thing," the bartender said. "They told me not to ask." Rumor has it that it's the carried over result of a stabbing in there years ago, or because the working ladies in the surrounding blocks would stop in for a quick fix. It's been a while since they've seen a knife or a pro in here though. "It used to be all shady," said the bartender. "There would be pimps over there, hookers over there. Now it's like Emerson kids and people before they hit the clubs."

"Now it's all hipsters." A recurring refrain.

TC's Lounge

1 Haviland St., Boston
Phone: 617-247-8109

Dive Bar Rating

🍾🍾🍾🍾🍾

If you were watching a ridiculous teen movie where the characters needed to make a stop in a dive bar—maybe they end up encountering some colorful characters that teach them a valuable life lesson, maybe it turns into a wacky drinking montage where one of the kids ends up with his pants off in the dumpster (haha, good one Hollywood!)—it would probably look a lot like TC's. The only problem with that is you wouldn't buy it. Your bullshit detector would be working over time. You'd think "Alright dude, we get it, this is a 'dive bar', you can tone it down with the kitschy décor and fluorescent bar signs and esoteric posters." It would look like they put together a collection of dive cliches to choose from, then just said "Screw it, put 'em all in. We need this place to read as 'dive' to the clueless rubes in flyover country." And yet TC's is very real. A little too real, actually.

Still, this is a classic dive, and its legions of fans, young and old, probably wouldn't have it any other way. They've got smokes and Cheezits for sale behind the bar, which you just don't see anywhere else, as well as baby jumpers emblazoned with "Future Customer" on the front. Shot specials like the Oxycontin shot and Liquid Cocaine are tempting, but you might want to stick with a bottle of beer. Wall after wall of Polaroids of decades of drinkers in various states of inebriation attest to its popularity across a wide swath of Boston bar culture. Here you've got your young professionals getting shitty after work, nearby Berklee musicians wasting away an evening that they should be practicing, and long-time regulars who might be vaguely perturbed by the gnat-like swarm of kids.

Following the trail of photos is sort of difficult, because this spot has a truly odd layout. There are three levels, and staircases that seem to come out of nowhere. It's like M.C. Escher's version of a dive. Booths along the bar side and in the back room give space to hang out, but the main section is dominated by an arcade. It's like a roadside carnival in here. Some of the customers look like they might have done well as carnies themselves.

Aside from photos, the walls and ceilings are papered with a truly awe-inspiring collection of old posters that give new meaning to the word random. Rebecca Romijn ass shot, DMX looking hard, a Mondale/

Ferraro campaign flyer. (!?) Some of the older ones are completely burnt out as well. That's probably from years of smoke. If you just stared at the ceiling you might think there had been a fire in this place at some point and they just built it back up around the damage because they couldn't bring themselves to throw out their beloved old decorations.

I've been here when it was absolutely mobbed with kids on a Thursday. Tonight, on a Monday, it's just me and four regulars watching *Seinfeld*. Against my better instincts I start laughing along with them. *Seinfeld*, of course, was notoriously the show about nothing. It's a weird contrast with TC's, the bar that's literally about everything.

Wally's Cafe
427 Massachusetts Ave., Boston
Phone: 617-424-1408

Take a minute to read the plaque outside this Mass Ave. jazz dive and you'll learn pretty much everything you need to know. "Last surviving reminder of Boston's jazz heyday," it reads. One of the first integrated venues, it was founded in 1947 by a Barbados immigrant named Joseph L. "Wally" Walcott when this area was the heart of the African American community in Boston. Charlie Parker, Billie Holliday and Art Blakey all performed here over the years, although almost anyone else on the rise in the jazz scene has stopped in at one point or another. It's easy to see why. Today its proximity to the Berklee College of Music makes it the prime training ground for the area's budding musicians, any of whom you can see laying it down 365 days of the year.

With that illustrious history you might think they'd have spent some time fixing up the joint, but it's remained largely unchanged over the decades. It's a cramped room, with an exposed brick wall on one side, very low ceilings, and a beat up old bar with two bright white lights illuminating the liquor on the shelves that is pretty much the only source of light in the room. The band, usually a trio or quartet—there's little room for anything much bigger—spill over from a tiny stage toward the back of the room, while patrons of all stripes listen attentively at the low slung cafe tables. There's little background noise. This is a place for listening to music, and listening hard, even if it is basically a shit hole. Everything besides the music is an afterthought.

Saturday night there's a Latin jazz quartet ripping it up. The female sax player is blowing like a goddamned whirlwind. The crowd is racially and generationally mixed, not as common as you might like in Boston, and definitely not something you would have seen back in the forties. Cute Berklee coeds are contemplating music theory at the next table, serious looking Asian professor types are ordering Duvels, and the old black neighborhood men are holding down the bar.

Amanda Palmer of the Dresden Dolls, about the closest thing

we've got to a contemporary iconic indie rock star in Boston right now, sums it up pretty well. "Most people who aren't in the neighborhood or Berklee types wouldn't deliberately head there," she says. "But that place is a joint. It's a serious joint."

The band is humming along on a wicked groove. The only thing missing is a blue haze of smoke curling through the air like a drawn out sax note. Before long they wind it down and the band leader announces that it's time for an open jam session. The crowd is full of anxious musicians assembling clarinets and unspooling guitar cables by now. It's for anyone who wants to play, he says. That's a pretty good way to describe the feel here for almost sixty years. Disparate players all thrown together on the fly and laying it down.

Pugliese's/ *(Luke O'Neil)*

CAMBRIDGE

The Cantab Lounge

738 Massachusetts Ave., Cambridge
Phone: 617-354-2685

Dive Bar Rating

It doesn't matter how many banks and cell phone stores and faux-industrial nightclub lofts you open here, Central Square is gentrification-proof. It's still a diverse neighborhood, both racially and economically speaking, and the bat shit insane homeless dudes and alcoholics clogging the sidewalks see to that.

The block the Cantab sits on seems particularly resilient to progress. There's a fancy sports bar next door, but there are also two indie book stores, if you can believe that. That's like finding a unicorn under a rainbow. There's a dive dry cleaners, a dive hardware store, dive convenience store, dive pizza shop and, this is 100% true, a dive dentist's office. There's also a ham sandwich in a plastic baggy just sitting out on the bench I'm on while I scribble all of this down. Of course there is. Down the block the omnipresent blue glow of flashing police lights flicker in and out of the shadows.

And then there's the Cantab, with its iconic green awning and stone facade. Big signs on the wall out front advertise the weekly lineup of bluegrass, jazz, local rock bands and the popular poetry slam nights. Blocking the entryway there's a near black out level drunk hesitating as if he's stuck deciding between going in and falling on his ass. He looks at me and waits for me to make the decision for us both. "You going in?" he asks. "I sure am."

Inside I find a squadron of his compatriots, black, white, hispanic, old and slightly less old bracing themselves against the bar and the cold alike – they're all still wearing their winter coats and hats. A lot of them look like the type of gentlemen who probably don't often have the convenience of removing their coats. This is the daytime side of the Cantab. At night, and in the downstairs bar you're more likely to find a music-going crowd. It's early enough now that the room still smells like last night's disinfectant scrub down.

The wobbly drunk zig zags off to the bathroom. "Is that Franky?" the bar man asks. Everyone chuckles. They've seen this little one act drama play out before. One nails his line. "He sure looked wonderful."

"He's not even supposed to be in here," the bartender says. He probably says that about a lot of these guys.

I asked James Caroline, who frequents and sometimes hosts the poetry slam downstairs here about some of his favorite characters to come through. "At its best it's a mix of townies, lamé-clad drag queens, grunge kids, punk bands, college kids, lost freaks, and quiet people who just wanted to hear something other than themselves," he says.

"Bono came down to read a poem and was not shown a lot of leniency," he said. "The attitude was apparently, 'Yeah you can sing, but can you write?' The longtime bartender here also threw George Thorogood out of the bar for standing on a table and playing his guitar one night. Threw him out. Didn't care who or what he was when people told her."

The bartender is asking Franky to leave now. Strangely they don't see eye to eye on this matter. Bartenders at a place like this have to have a firm but tender hand. A drunk man shut off at a bar reverts to a petulant, child-like state. Drinking, of course, is often about lowering your inhibitions and acting like a younger version of yourself. Feels good most of the time. That doesn't mean it looks pretty to someone watching. That about sums up the Cantab too.

Charlie's Kitchen

10 Eliot St., Cambridge
Phone: 617-492-9646

One quick way to determine the authenticity of any given dive is by a quick survey of the tattoos on display both behind and seated at the bar. The bigger the ratio of faded-greenish naval tattoos to pretty flower shoulder sleeves the closer you get to the type of proud shit hole you can call a real dive. Things definitely skew toward the latter at Charlie's, although this Cambridge institution more than makes up for a scenester aura with its forty years in the trenches pulling cheap beers, grilling up surprisingly decent food and, from the looks of it, never once updating the interior décor.

The downstairs bar has a sort of rockabilly diner vibe and a truly random collection of accumulated bar detritus – dusty mirrors, old beer signs and the like. It's the type of old-timey restaurant you could imagine your mother working at, serving up hamburgers on roller skates when she was young. On second thought, don't imagine that.

They've also got big cans of Rolling Rock for $3.50, which is surprising, because who knew they even still made that beer? Upstairs pulls in the choppy bangs and skinny black jeans crowd alongside slumming students with its karaoke nights, the occasional live punk band and the type of curated jukebox (Bad Brains, Slap Shot, The Clash, Morphine, The Smiths) that covers all of the indie, punk and Boston-centric bases, and inspires rapture from devotees who hover around it like a shrine.

Outside, the urban oasis of the beer garden brings in a complete cross-spectrum of Cambridge nightlife during the summer. And while it's a great spot for a beer, unless I find myself hopelessly lost in some slum in Munich or whatever (happens more than you'd think) I don't really want to associate the words beer and garden with my dive bars. Add to that its kitschy neon signs advertising burger specials and the sometimes insufferably affected clientele (like me, for example) and it'd be tempting to dismiss Charlie's as a sort simulacrum of a "dive," but one glance at the ceilings scarred brown by years of smoke and you realize this is the type of place that's seen, and served, them all. George Bush used to toss them back here back in his Harvard days apparently, which probably doesn't sound like much of a recommendation at first, but keep in mind getting shit-faced was pretty much the only thing that dude ever really figured out how to do right.

The Courtside Restaurant and Pub

Dive Bar Rating

291 Cambridge St., Cambridge
Phone: 617-547-4374

Today it's known as a karaoke mecca for ironic post-college dive-goers after their softball games, but when the Alberts family first opened it up in 1943 as the A&S Cafe it was a quintessential example of the era's neighborhood bar. John Alberts was born that same year, and he's been working at the bar pretty much ever since.

He started back in 1962 he says. A lot has changed since then. "We're still a neighborhood bar, but the neighborhood has changed. As has every neighborhood in the city. In this area here, luckily we always had the [Middlesex Superior Court] house, now we don't of course."

"There were factories all over the place," he remembers. Chocolate factories, sausage factories, casket factories. "It was all factories and all the people that lived in this area they either worked in the courthouse or the factories." The bar's proximity to the court is where it gets its name. "We used to feed the juries, they used to bring them over here at lunch time."

Another big change? When he first started here there were no women in the bars, Alberts says. "People don't realize it, but it wasn't until the late sixties, early seventies when you'd find a woman in a bar. Women used to tap on the window and they'd say 'Hey Luke your wife's out there.'"

"Sometime in the seventies women's lib started to come around and when women came in they had women's drinks that they drank. Women did not drink shots and beers. They drank Pink Lady's and Sombreros. Basically when light beer first came out, that's when women started drinking beer. When light beer came out with their ads they had to incorporate athletes – light beer was like a sissy's beer. That's when women started drinking beer. Now you go in and women are drinking shots and beer. But that's the way it was."

They certainly don't have a problem drinking here today. The biker chick I saw warbling her way though Guns N Roses karaoke a while back and the giggling groups of college girls doing Journey songs are a testament to that.

The Courtside Restaurant and Pub

They didn't have seats at bars when he first started either Alberts says, continuing the history lesson. "You had a railing and you stood and put your foot up on a rail. Bar stools came in about the sixties too. They stood at bars and leaned at the bar." No credit cards either. "Every neighborhood bar had a book and people had tabs. And when they got paid they would come in and pay off the bar tab. Of course in those days they'd run up a tab at one bar and then go down and drink at the next one."

All the kids that come in now certainly have credit cards, probably plenty of money on them too.

It's probably better for business that way.

Then again, maybe it isn't.

"In the old days you had what you called regulars, you knew that this guy came in every day when he got off work. There used to be night shifts that worked at the court house. They'd all go in before the shift at eleven, then come back the next morning when we opened." In those days everyone drank at lunch too. "Judges, lawyers, juries. Lawyers would come in in the morning with their clients. It's a way of life change. People don't drink at lunch anymore. It's become taboo. That's a big difference too. I think people go to health clubs at lunch, but they don't go and drink at lunch anymore. Times change. That's the way of life."

(*Luke O'Neil*)

Joey Mac's

23 Warren St., Cambridge
No phone

Dive Bar Rating

One of the first establishments to receive a liquor license from the city of Cambridge in the 1930s, this spot has been haunted by the entire spectrum of city characters over the decades, some high, some low, and some in between. One who you may have heard of by the name John F. Kennedy, stopped in in 1958 on a whirlwind campaign jag. An old account in the *Harvard Crimson* reads: "Councilor Alfred E. Vellucci and Senator John F. Kennedy '40 shared a 'real Italian dinner' last night in a crowded East Cambridge restaurant." It would be almost impossible to imagine Kennedy, or any other politician for that matter, coming through here now. He'd be kicked off the ticket.

Opened by Salvatore Macarelli in the 1930s, it used to be a more respectable restaurant, serving many of the area's Italian immigrants. Somewhere along the line he changed the name to Joey Mac's, then to Macacrelli and Sons. In later years it was owned by Thomas R. Ryan Jr., a bookie who spent almost two years in jail for refusing to rat out James "Whitey" Bulger and Stephen "The Rifleman" Flemmi. Probably a good idea at the time. Ryan would find himself jammed up again in a drug sting a few years back.

Today the reputation for a seediness still hangs over the bar like a cloud, but it's pretty much undeserved. The side street it's located on is a bit spooky however. Faceless three story houses, chain link fences demarcating yards of nothing, and an ominous tenement in the near distance add an air of blighted isolation. While it's still largely a locals bar, none of that has dissuaded the dive-hunting twenty somethings who've discovered it. That's evidenced by the array of video games, trivia nights, a pool table, karaoke and the usual lineup of bullshit pseudo events designed to give people an excuse to distract themselves from the drinking they're doing to distract themselves.

I felt right at home when I came here. A little too at home, by the way. The people at these dives are going to have to stop being so friendly, or else I'll have to rethink my whole stereotype. They'd just ordered some pizzas and the bartender offered me a slice.

"Damn it, now it's gonna take longer to get buzzed!" one of the middle aged locals rasped.

My friends Leah and Mike expected to get trouble when they came in last. She sums it up pretty nicely. "There was about fifteen people in there, all townies over forty," she told me. "We got many, many stares. But we played pool and talked to some old guys. The woman working behind the bar was like sixty. I'll always remember she was sticking her hand in a huge bag of pretzels and serving them in a bowl and she saw that we were staring and she says 'I just washed my hands heh heh' in her smoker's cough voice. We ended up smoking weed with some townie guys that were around our age before we left sneaking out a few Miller High Lifes. It's a pretty rugged place but a nice chill spot and cheap. I liked that we didn't get fucked-with which we thought would happen from all the stares. I'm sure you can find many mystical people and things in there."

I do. I spot one of the regulars I just encountered at Pugs around the corner. He's got a rat tail, shaved head, a Bruins jacket and some sort of impenetrable brogue. When the Bruins score his friend starts chanting "Jager bombs! Jager bombs!" and points at everyone in the bar. I pass this time. The bartender does a shot with her friends.

"It doesn't make me a bad girl," she says. "Just a fun one."

Newtowne Grille

1945 Massachusetts Ave., Cambridge
Phone: 617-661-0706

Dive Bar Rating

Taking your city's history for granted is too easy. It's pretty rare that you find yourself walking down the streets you've been on hundreds of times and thinking, "I wonder what this place looked like 100 or 50, or even 20 years ago." Odds are, unless you live in some still forgotten corner of the universe untouched by civilization, it didn't look anything like it does now. Dives are essential because many of them carry that history over. At their best they're like little time capsules from the past that we get to reopen again and again every time we belly up for a pint. In the case of the Newtowne Pub you do get some sense of the old working class Porter Square, although it's certainly become modernized and popular amongst the young generation of nearby Tufts and Lesley students, and it's probably unlikely that they had this many flatscreen TVs back in 1966 when this place opened, but you get the idea.

You can also find some literal evidence of what the old neighborhood was like if you scan the walls. Framed black and white photos open a window onto Porter in the 1920s. The train ran above ground here then. It still looks like traffic was a bitch then too though.

Today Porter is a curious neighborhood. It straddles the line between relatively working class Somerville on the one side, and the blocks adjacent to Mass Ave. lined with beautiful Victorians home to the bevy of academics from nearby schools. Sorry, red state America, this is probably ground zero for everything you hate about the liberal elites.

Today the bar is a whirlwind of clutter, but collected in a sort of harmony. Bright red walls are decked out in sports memorabilia of course, and the room is circled by low, long, retro diner style booths. You'll find a mix of college kids scarfing down pizza, dudes in Celtics tank tops and shorts (in January, by the way), elderly couples eating out in the only way they really know how anymore, and a cast of local working men talking shit around the bar.

If a lot of dives are the equivalent of a sickly 80 year old, this one is more of a robust 40, even if it is actually older than that. There's life in here. A ruddy glow of relative health. Even the group of twenty octogenarians in tuxedos sitting down to eat for a wedding or class reunion or whatever were buoyant and full of energy. Tuxedos are probably a rare occurrence in here I'm guessing. My friends brought their two month old baby in to watch the Patriots with a group of our friends the other week. So there's your age span here: two months to ancient. "Last time I was here I saw a 60 year old woman with her tits hanging out dancing to "My Humps" one of them told me.

"It's got a much more friendly vibe because of where it is," Michelle my girlfriend says while we sip our beers at the bar. "In a square that's 100 percent gentrified it's much less intimidating than other dives. Anyone could walk into this place and feel comfortable," she says. "Well, maybe not in heels and a mini skirt."

"The regulars don't seem as hardened," she went on. "Just the fact of where they are, they probably have it a little bit better than some of these other dives we've been to." She's got a point. Being here, unlike some of the other bars in this book, doesn't make you want to die. It makes you want to live. At least long enough for another $3 beer anyway.

Paddy's Lunch

260 Walden St., Cambridge
Phone: 617-547-8739

A small residential building in a quiet residential neighborhood doesn't seem a likely location for a bar. Maybe a busy little laundromat, or a poorly stocked bodega, but a bar? One that's been there for over seventy five years? A quick scan of the brightly lit room on a crowded Saturday night, where the crowd has thrown their coats on all the tables and the backs of all the chairs chairs so a newcomer has to stand in the middle of the room like an asshole, and it all begins to make sense. It's more like a family get together than a place of business.

"In 1934 my grandfather started it," owner Ruth Allen tells me. "Patrick Fennell. They called him Paddy. He got laid off from the Boston elevated, the old MBTA, and my grandmother actually ran it from the forties and fifties until she died in 1960. Then my mum ran it from then until about ten years ago, and I've had it since then. It's considered a men's bar, but it's run by women that's the funny part."

"Back then my grandmother would stop serving the guys between twelve and one, and she'd turn on the rosary. Everyone knew that they'd better get their beer before twelve or else they wouldn't have one."

The neighborhood has gone through ebbs and tides over the decades, she says. In the fifties through seventies it was still a middle class stronghold here. "Paddy's was looked at by the neighborhood as the place you went to talk to people that knew your parents and grandparents. In the sixties and seventies, the neighborhood kind of looked down on Paddy's—the people who were buying the houses, the professors and stuff. But there was a group of professors who came from the middle class who took pride in Paddy's because it was a place that they felt comfortable."

Eventually her parents started having political events at the bar. Long time Speaker of the House Tip O'Neil used to play cards in the back room with Judge Sullivan in the back of Paddy's. John Kennedy came in when he was running. Joe Kennedy too, on a tour of places where his uncle started. "We had the true Kennedy political machine here. Then they started saying 'What a great place, it's just like regular people.' We were like 'Yeah, well, we don't think of it as a place with regular people!'

The nineties were tough, with a lot of people purchasing homes in the neighborhood to resell them. Paddy's was a respite for the ones who were left, at which point it became almost like a private club, she says. That explains the less than welcoming reception I got. I don't blame them though. Who am I anyway? "It was always sort of like, why are you here?' sort of thing" she says. You've got to earn your spot at the bar.

My friend Jennifer felt intimidated by the demeanor when she first moved into the area. "We were so excited to have a local pub across the street and we thought we'd go all the time," she tells me. "As soon as we mentioned the name Paddy's to people their response was consistently 'Don't go there! You have to know someone to get in.'"

"It took nearly a year and a half before we had the courage to venture in without knowing a soul. To our surprise we had a great time. The bartenders and regulars have got to be some of the nicest people we've met in Cambridge."

Friends and being nice don't necessarily pay the bills though. It's hard to keep a place like this in business these days. "We were lucky that my parents bought the place when they did otherwise we wouldn't be here anymore," Ruth says. She just raised the price of a beer from $3 to $3.50 and there was an uproar. It wouldn't be family in Massachusetts if there weren't a little in-fighting though.

Portugalia

723 Cambridge St., Cambridge
Phone: 617-491-5373

Dive Bar Rating

Drive up and down Cambridge St., and the impact of the Portuguese character of the area becomes evident. Groceries, butchers, restaurants and bars, many of which cater specifically to the Portuguese community, jump out from every corner. Some, like Portuglia, are a little harder to find. Although it's renowned for its Northern Portugal cuisine, particularly its salt colds, the bar side is practically unheard of even though it's been here some fifteen years. I literally stumbled across it by accident on my way from Pug's to Joey Mac's on a freezing Saturday night looking for respite from the cold. While the food here may be respected, the bar is like a portal into another country's version of the dive bar.

The room is bright, but not in the usual dive bar heat lamp fashion. The Mediterranean style architecture features striking colors, woods and tiles along the walls. Golden tinted tin behind the bar gives off a wave of reflective light. A group of Portuguese and Brazilian regulars are passing time arguing about the upcoming World Cup match between their two sides coming later that summer. The record didn't exactly scratch when I walked in, but it was about to. Ilda behind the bar quickly wrapped me up in her warm embrace and ushered me to a seat in such a friendly way it was almost as if she was worried about me.

"What brings you in on this cold winter night?" she asked, which was either concern or threatening. Then she asked for my name. "It's pretty low key in here, Luke." It's never good when someone uses your name in a sentence.

I order a Bud Light and a bag of chips, $3.50. She's pretty insistent on getting me a plate for my tiny bag of ruffles, but I demur. After a minute I think better of refusing the offer. They've got great food here, she tells me, and I believe her. The restaurant is around the other side, with a few families eating a late dinner. That explains how I almost knocked over a little child on my way to the bathroom. Sometimes when you wander into a place like this that isn't as surprising as you'd think. It's like the usual rules don't apply. For example, it's perfectly acceptable at a dive bar to stare at someone like they just took your shit apparently. The only other white guy in the room seems to think I've uncovered his secret. Ilda is laying down the rules of one kind though. One of the kids from the restaurant is trying to pull a fast one and get a beer for his underage friend. No way. Not on her watch. To be honest I'm not sure if I want her to be my mother or my girlfriend. She's at that indeterminate European age that could be almost anything.

The crowd at the bar turns out to be toothless. In some cases literally. There is little English to be heard. Ilda passes around a bowl of bar cherries, which unsurprisingly, elicits some risque comments from the old timers at the bar. "Have you ever had one?" she asks me. Everyone's looking now. "Um. No, this is my first time," I say. It's not funny, but it gets a laugh. And just like this I'm a regular now. Seconds later I'm old news, a plant in the corner, left alone to my own devices by the Keno machine. World Cup talk again. "I hate Brazil," the toothless guy says to his friend. "And I hate Portugal."

(Luke O'Neil)

Pugliese Bar & Grill

635 Cambridge St., Cambridge
Phone: 617-491-9616

Dive Bar Rating

During the latter part of the 19th century East Cambridge was a main industrial center of the city. Furniture and glass factories abounded making use of the close proximity to Boston and the nearby Charles River. During that time it was a major landing point for many Irish immigrants, and towards the turn of the century an influx of Italian and Portuguese as well. That same proximity to Boston – you can see the city skyline just over the Charles—has made it a prime location for the development of luxury high rise condos, some of which have been built out of those same factories responsible for the neighborhood's birth. Gentrification still hasn't swept the area clean however, and despite the sobering commercial anchor of the Cambridgeside Galleria mall, it's still one of the higher crime rate areas in Cambridge.

Evidence of its historical diversity exists as well in the wealth of dive bars up and down Cambridge St., and the preponderance of Portuguese businesses, restaurants and bars. You can read the history of East Cambridge in the progression of Pugs over the years. It's been called Pugliese's since 1933, but before that time the bar stood as a joint called Madden's. A large blown up black and white photo on the wall shows owner Dan Madden on Old Home Day 1906 with the bar decked out in draping American flags. Even back then it was important for immigrants to make outward displays of patriotism it seems.

Today it's a reliable neighborhood bar for a diverse crowd of old and young alike. Mostly old. They underwent a significant remodeling about five years ago, moving from run down dive ideal to slightly spruced up dive.

"The neighborhood has gone through a lot of changes over the years," John the bartender says. He grew up in nearby Winter Hill in Somerville. "It was a Portuguese neighborhood originally. Most of the places on the street are Portuguese, but some of them are going Brazilian because there's a close connection."

Lynard Skynard is blasting on the juke while we talk. "For the most part the crowd here is older," he says. "We get a lot of regulars that have been regulars here since before I was born. The neighborhood is changing though. It's getting younger. It's interesting to see the changes and to see the twenty year olds interact with the seventy year olds."

One of the regulars asks John to throw a game of darts. "You're gonna get your ass kicked," the challenger says. He's wearing a black leather Aerosmith jacket. It's a friendly boast though, in a friendly room, despite the seeming air of indifference from the regulars. Probably the only ass kicking that will go down here tonight, unless they start pulling the handle on that Jagermeister machine a lot more frequently.

"It's chill in here," says Rachel, taking over behind the bar. "Rare that anyone isn't well behaved. I don't even remember the last fight. A year ago? The people are good here, even if new people come in they talk to them right off the bat."

An Andy Warhol type and a punchy British bloke with a nose that's seen some fist work anchor the bar. Odd couple. The Aerosmith fan is loading the juke with country cock rock with his girlfriend, or sister, or mother. It's easy to lose all sense of social standing and relationship status in a place like this. Who the hell can tell who anyone is and what they mean to each other. That's the point. No one cares.

Riverside Pizza

305 River St., Cambridge
Phone: 617-354-8800

Relocate this bar into any other neighborhood, maybe even a few blocks over, and it would look much like literally any other dive you'll find in Cambridge. But demographics, and history, have a way of transforming the makeup of a crowd. At Riverside, one half take out pizza shop, one half dive bar, its pedigree as a largely African American watering hole, particularly when it was known as Guertin's twenty years or so back, continues to this day.

In the Boston area, race is nowhere near as in your face as the stereotype outside of Massachusetts, or our dubious past might indicate, but bars are still relatively segregated. This is a decidedly black dive, and aside from the makeup of the crowd, there are a few subtle reminders of that here. The r&b and classic funk soundtrack for one; framed black and white portraits of Etta James and Louis Armstrong on the walls too. Not so common in your typical Irish joint. Of course they're sharing space with tributes to Bobby Orr and other Boston sports icons, don't forget we're in greater Boston after all, where sports transcend all. Like tonight, for example, with the NCAA tournament playing out on one of the bar's antiquated TV boxes hung over the bar. (There is one newer model as well, but strangely no one is paying attention to that one.)

A young dude in dreads at the bar is yelling at the game. "He can't hear you," his girlfriend shouts back. "You're like Don King!" comes a voice from across the room "Whoever is up you're with." I don't get it.

I'm stashed into the corner watching the game myself, losing on my picks as usual. There's a towering pile of empty beer boxes threatening to topple over near me. It's like a metaphor for my gambling career. A middled aged man in a fedora and scarf is pacing back and forth nervously and getting up and down from his bar stool every thirty seconds. He's drinking a Heineken and a Hennessey (come on dude) and has a lot riding on the Keno numbers. Up $300 so far today he tells me. Across the room a few old Italian guys with wrinkles as deep as the nearby Charles River are taking it all in quietly.

"I get food for takeout here sometimes," a guy who lives nearby tells me. "The bar is a neighborhood shit hole. They only have Bud bottles and it is full of people who are either on drugs or Keno gambling." Yup, I'd say that counts as a dive.

Kentucky is losing to West Virgina. "Stick a fork in Kentucky! The Colonel is done!" the animated guy yells. He's working the crowd like a hype man. I'm counting my losses as the smell of fried cheese wafts in from the attached restaurant side. A three generation deep family are eating next to me at the bar, granddad on down. If you stay here drinking late enough the owners will bring over a few free pies at the end of the night. Family. Generosity. Community.

Speaking of which: across the street are some newly built condos for sale, white picket fence and all. You can change the look of the place, but sometimes the sense of community lingers a little while longer all the same.

(Luke O'Neil)

CAMBRIDGE

BOSTON'S BEST DIVE BARS

Whitney's Cafe

37 JFK St., Cambridge
Phone: 617-354-8172

Dive Bar Rating

The neighborhood where you find any given dive bar is clearly going to have an influence on the bar's demographic. Put a dive downtown and it's going to attract cubicle types pretending they don't hate their lives before the miserable commute home. Throw it in a blighted neighborhood and it's going to have a higher potential for crime. And with a bar like Whitney's located in the student bastion of Harvard Square, you're going to find a more collegiate demeanor (aka young douches.)

Youth complicates a dive bar. Fresh-faced drinkers, even at their rowdiest, fill in the messy cracks of a dive bar's dirty facade. It's like a forty year old putting makeup on, except in this case the makeup is a twenty three year old Long Island transplant liberal arts major and his loud girlfriend, and the face is a square box room with puddles of beer in the pisser.

People have been complaining about the corporate makeover of Harvard Square for so long now it becomes harder every passing year to remember exactly what all the fuss was about in the first place. If you believe the nostalgia-minded (aka old people), cheap beer flowed freely through the streets and magical hamburgers served in gritty restaurants with character went for a half nickel. The well-heeled influence of the academic behemoth around the corner has certainly had a depressingly homogenizing effect on neighborhood business though, turning the area into a sort of open air mall food court. But if you want a taste of what things might well have been like "back in the day" Whitney's serves as a close-enough anachronistic reminder.

Hidden in plain site on the main throughway of the square, it's the type of innocuous bar people who work in the neighborhood could walk by on their lunch break every day for years and never even notice. They may, however, smell it. Don't be fooled by the expensive looking flat screen TVs mounted on the walls here (almost a requirement in sports-crazy Boston), you know you're in a dive when that sweet au de toilette smacks you in the face on the way in the door. Fluorescent beer signs, a well-maintained dart board, internet juke box, Buck Hunter and cheap Bud on tap make this a near complete dive-bar bingo. Even with those student-tempting staples and its locale well within hurling distance of the nearby dorms, don't be surprised to find a reasonable share of burly goateed types with their denim-tuxedoed lady friends throwing back PBR at the bar. Although the conspicuous lack of a regular hipster clientele despite the presence of an Urban Outfitters next door is either a testament to Whitney's dive bonafides, or a condemnation of its irrelevance, depending on how many Pixies records you've got on your Ipod.

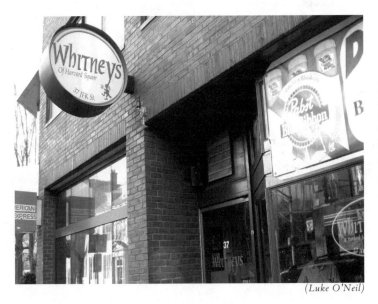

(Luke O'Neil)

Best Dive Bars by College

Emerson • The Tam, Remmington's

Harvard • Whitney's, Charlie's Kitchen

MIT • The Thirsty Ear Pub

Tufts • Sligo

Boston University • The Dugout

Boston College • The Last Drop, Mary Ann's

Berklee • TC's, Wally's Cafe

Northeastern • Punter's Pub, Our House East

Suffolk • Sidebar

CHARLESTOWN/NORTH END

Corner Cafe

87 Prince St., Boston
Phone: 617-523-8997

Dive Bar Rating

"It's a locals haven, with lots of vowels and hand movements," my co-worker Rudy tells me when I ask about what to expect at the Corner Cafe. He should know, he's lived in this North End neighborhood for fifty years. Also, he's Italian, so, you know, it's not racist.

"There's lots of Marias and Tonys, decades of choice in the jukebox, cheap drinks, and best of all, a scratch ticket machine." Sounds like a dive bar; doesn't sound much like the North End.

The North End is one of the most historic areas in the city, and its cramped, cobblestone streets are littered with all sorts of architectural history you've probably forgotten from grade school American Revolution lessons. (Do they still teach kids about that shit in school anymore?) Landmarks like the Old North Church and Paul Revere House bring tourists in by the droves every summer to hump along the Freedom Trail. But guess what, this dive bar book is your new Freedom Trail. Freedom from over-priced bars without character. You'll find plenty of those around here; it's a small neighborhood, but there's something like 100 restaurants. Most of them are precious, candle-lit romantic Italian bistros that are indistinguishable from one another. There are also cute little gelato shops, ristorantes, brick oven pizza shops and brick oven walk-up apartments. It would make a great set for a film about Italian American gangsters in the sixties trying to go straight and open their own pizza shop if the streets weren't already so cramped. There's no room to park those giant lighting rigs. Ben Affleck still managed to stage a pretty awesome claustrophobic car chase in *The Town* on these tiny streets though, which I'm still marveling at.

There's no room for much of anything inside this North End dive either, one of the only of its kind around. The bar is small, seating about eight, and there are a few tables scattered about. The mirrors on the walls don't do much to make it seem like a larger space. Rudy's right, this is a haven; a place for neighborhood lifers to get away from the tourists. They aren't always successful though. For every cannoli-fisted old timer who ducks in here, there's a selection of other assorted archetypes. Drunk suits, muscle-bound guidos, crack heads in basketball tank tops in the winter, college age girls, striking, and strikingly abrasive North End women, and neighborhood dogs (who move their paws then they bark) all packed into a tiny little corner pub.

Sit down at the bar and you might immediately find yourself talking to an old townie, a business man from some weird suburb like Weston and a bouncer-looking guy in a tight black t-shirt who somehow all seem to have become best friends over a couple beers. They'll want to know what your accent is, because people in bars like this need to be able to place others into categories of geographical origin. It helps makes sense of the world. Is it British? No, you'll say. You've spent so much time trying to downplay your retarded Boston accent that you wound up with this weird affectation. Besides they kicked the British out of this neighborhood a couple hundred years ago.

Just Like The Movies

Doyle's Cafe *Mystic River*

Old Sully's *The Town*

Daisy Buchanan's *The Company Men*

Jacob Wirth *Knight and Day*

Murphy's Law *Gone Baby Gone*, *The Maiden Heist*

Cataloni's *Gone Baby Gone*

Durty Nelly's

108 Blackstone St., Boston
Phone: 617-742-2090

Dive Bar Rating

As the story goes, this Haymarket bar was named after an old market keeper from owner Joe Somers' home town in Cork City, Ireland by the name of Nelly. She wore an old shawl every day that she never bothered to clean. What's the point when it's only going to get dirty again, she'd say. You can't really argue with that logic. That's the type of thinking that keeps most of our beloved dive bars in tatters themselves.

This faux-cutesy pub overlooking the Greenway, and on the back end of Faneuil Hall, underwent a remodeling a few years ago, but they didn't clean the shawl entirely. Unlike Somers' other Irish pubs in the area, the Green Dragon, Mr. Dooley's, Hooley House and Hennesy's, all of which are basically tourist traps and Irish-themed pissing holes for recent college grads who haven't figured out how to act like adults yet, Durty Nelly's is just, well, dirty enough to maintain its bonafides. It resists the pub on steroids feel of much of the surrounding area, and after stumbling over here from a disappointing trip to the Point, a bar I was considering including before I saw all the tourist families watching a guy with an acoustic sing a Backstreet Boys song, it's a stark contrast.

The tourism industry in the Haymarket area can whitewash even the oldest historic bars into oblivion. Nelly's keeps a messier house. There's a dusty air settling over the books and tea-cups lining the shelves on the walls. Candelabras and washed-out black and white photos lend a touch of authenticity. The room is small and cramped and you're basically forced to talk to the person sitting next to you, which is one of the best, and worst, things about dive bars and Irish pubs in general. You're either going to get a real psycho, or the cutest old guy you ever met. You might find ten laborer types drinking away the afternoon as well, or an old drunk in a tank top and flip flops all trying their best not to lose their shit over two moderately attractive young women who've set up shop at the bar here.

Somers bought the place about five years ago. It used to be called Pete's, an old timer with a snake tattoo and a Marine's bearing named

Pat tells me. He wants to talk about his history here pretty bad, but no one is paying attention to him. The girls are sucking all the attention into their perfumed vortex of flirtation.

Since the smoking ban, a lot of guys like him stopped coming out at all, Pat says. They're missing out. You can step outside here, walk across the street to the Greenway and take in the sea air and beautiful view of the North End and have all the smoke you want between pints.

Back in the bar an old black guy with a personal Red Sox cozy around his beer is drawing tattoo-style art in full color on bar napkins. He's been coming here for as long as he can remember too, he says. It's quiet mostly, and he likes his spot in the corner. Next to him a guy in a Hawaiian shirt and hair that looks like a frightened clown's wig is buying shots for the girls. Look, I like a hot chick as much as the next guy, but come on ladies... You're making everyone tense. This is a place where people go day by day to forget their troubles, not to be reminded with every floral scented swish of your luxurious hair that they are never going to touch anyone like you ever again. Then again, who knows, the way the shots are going things could end up getting dirty in here. I wonder what Nelly would say about that?

Four Winds Bar and Grille

266 Commercial St., Boston
Phone: 617-742-3922

Dive Bar Rating

The city of Boston is notoriously tight-fisted with its distribution of liquor licenses. For people looking to open new bars or restaurants, procuring one is often more of an impediment to opening than coming up with the hundreds of thousands of dollars it takes to actually start the business. I bring that up in regards to Four Winds because it's a good example of one of the reasons bars like this can actually stay in business. With the way that licenses are awarded in the city, it's almost impossible to open a new bar with a 2 a.m. closing time. You basically can't even open a bar anymore unless you're also selling food. But bars that have been grandfathered in with longstanding licenses can thrive if they play their cards right.

Not that this Italian restaurant by way of sports dive at the foot of the North End is doing gangbusters. But since they're the only bar in the area with a late closing time, they're the last call spot of choice for the neighborhood's legion of restaurant workers. Business, as they say, is business. And restaurant industry folks can sure drink.

"It's the diviest place in the North End," my friend Jason told me. He used to bartend there not too long ago. We were talking while trapped on a roof deck in the North End because one of his friends had locked us up here by accident. Long story, but all things considered, it wasn't such a bad place to be. We had hot dogs, beer and cigarettes and lots of dive bars to talk about. Although if help hadn't arrive as soon as it did I was seriously considering pulling some Spiderman shit.

"You've got dirtbags there drinking by day. And at night it's anyone from underage kids to serious scumbags." What's the difference between a scumbag and a dirtbag? I forgot to ask. "There's always puke on the bathroom too," he told me.

The Four Winds doesn't look as bad as all that. With its threadbare rug and sturdy wooden, sea-side décor – you can see the water from the bar – it looks like an Italian joint that just let itself go. The humid air coming off the water by Sargents Wharf isn't exactly doing wonders for the smell in here though, or for the sticky bar top, but you could do worse. Just not anywhere nearby. The restaurants and bars around here are all cute candle-lit enotecas.

A couple of Euros wander in while I'm swilling back an ill-advised Sam Adams at the bar after I finally make my way off Jason's roof. They're looking for espresso. The bartender, a sturdy, ironic blonde thinks it's the most hilarious thing ever. There's a Starbucks right across the street. "Does this look like the type of place that has espresso!?" she mumbles after they leave. "Fucking tourists."

Well, she has a point, tourists are insufferable. But come on, this is the North End. Espresso runs through its veins. Bev, the older bar-marm who worked here forever isn't in tonight. She's been here so long many of the regulars started calling her mom. The rest of the crew is sort of a surly lot, but if you had to deal with clueless tourists and last-call hustling drunks at the end of the night, you'd get a little heated yourself. Besides, being a short-tempered douche is kind of like an Italian heritage thing, right? What's more North End appropriate than that?

Old Sully's

56 Union St., Charlestown
No phone

Dive Bar Rating

Tacked onto the back end of a residential building, all brown weathered shingles and distinguished only by the shredded American flags tacked to the outside walls, Sully's is at the bottom of a hill called "the valley" that leads back toward the more, say, civilized part of the Town. It's as if the neighborhood is shrugging its shoulders and trying to send it rolling off the hill into the nowhere land that separates it from Boston. It won't be so easy to get rid of though, rapidly-rising property values notwithstanding. The bar has been here since Prohibition, when Dan Sullivan, the late owner, started serving drinks in secret. The family still maintains the bar in the same spirit: it's largely for people in the know, who can actually find it. And although the bar scene in Charlestown has been decimated over the decades, it still serves as a respite for old neighborhood guys, union workers, Logan Airport police, and shifty, fast-talking guys in gold chains who retire here for a big sip of the familiar.

What they're met with inside is an old clubhouse style, lunch-counter room. The bar is worn, orange formica, the tile floor is chipped. The walls are a dusty, old, forgotten wing of the museum of Charlestown, with framed photos of regulars gone-by and notable Boston tipplers like JFK, who is said to have stopped in here in the 60s. Seems like he stopped into most of these really old dives actually. They sure campaigned differently back then. Thinking about Obama or some Republican turd coming in here now is a joke.

When you walk in all the heads turn. They have to, because the room is so small you practically land right in the middle of a conversation. Be ready to talk too, the swiveling bar stools are so close together, and there are so few of them, it would be weird if you didn't strike up a conversation with the guy next to you. I thought I might get the cold shoulder when I came in, and I did at first. Jimmy the bartender was a little suspicious, but he warmed soon. It didn't hurt that a loud gay couple came in after me that ended up seeming more out of place than I was, taking the heat off me.

"It's exactly the type of bar that Hollywood has been looking for around Boston for the last few years," says Glenn Yoder, my colleague at the Globe. Coincidentally, they seem to have found it. Ben Affleck filmed scenes here inside and out for his film "The Town" about, you guessed it, blue-collar Boston toughs torn between loyalty and bla bla bla. Blake Lively's character in the film has a telling line: "All these yuppies here think there's no more serious white people in Charlestown." But then again, the character is fucked up on oxies the whole movie, so, you know, keep that in mind.

"For me, its authenticity stood out," says Yoder. "It was one of the first bars I went to in Boston, and I half expected them all to be that way. Honestly, I haven't found too many like it."

That's because there aren't. Back inside, the talk turns to whiskey. They don't carry Makers Mark, or Wild Turkey here. "We're old school here," Jimmy the bartender says. That's an understatement. There's an 8-track player behind the bar. A phone booth is the only phone line. There's a back area here that's like a function room of sorts. I'm getting a little too excited about the football on the TV and everyone else is indifferent. It's probably the only time I can think of where I felt like it was more appropriate to feign disinterest in football in a Boston dive. Is football not tough anymore?

Dan, one of the guys sitting next to me wants to talk about playing football in high school though. He's from Ohio, a big time school. Not me, we lost every single game we ever played, I said. He and his boyfriend are some sort of higher-ups in the Boy Scouts organization. Unsurprisingly, they don't see eye to eye with a lot of the policies of that Republican in training operation. "We're just waiting for the older regime to die off," he says. "It's the same thing in places like Syria and other countries. They just want the old guard to die off." The exact opposite sentiment applies to bars like this.

Sullivan's Pub

85 Main St., Charlestown
Phone: 617-242-3222

Dive Bar Rating

Because of Charlestown's illustrious history—it was the original capital of Massachusetts, and home to a number of important landmarks like the Bunker Hill Monument and the USS Constitution —you'd be surprised to find a dive bar along these closely packed streets amidst so many gorgeous Colonial era buildings. But Sully's persists. New Sully's, rather. It's called that because it's owned by the same family as the much older, prohibition-era Old Sully's just around the corner. I was surprised to find it myself and I was actually looking for it. Walking along the charmingly cramped streets of the neighborhood my girlfriend and I came across a home that literally stopped us in our tracks. A gorgeous Colonial townhouse with the type of lavishly landscaped garden you'd see in Martha Stewart's magazine or something. We gawked. A woman who looked like money on legs was having an argument on the phone by the finely crafted stone pools. One of the pools. Anyway, Sully's is on the next block over.

The bar here has been open for forty three years, the bartender tells us, pointing to a photo on the wall of what it looked like when her father bought it back then. It used to be a soda shoppe. The rows of schwag booze behind the bar seem chosen to replicate that old fashioned soda fountain vibe from the photo: root beer, vanilla and butterscotch schnapps. Purple something. It's a collection of dive liquor, all generic, giant plastic jugs that look like they should have questions marks affixed to their logos. Arrow Coffee Flavored "Brandy"? Sutton Club "Gin"?

The room is collection of standard dive signifiers: beat up tile floors, drop tile ceilings, mounted fish and framed black and white photos. The stained glass shamrock windows are a nice touch. Michelle thinks it's a little too clean in here. Perhaps, but they've had their share of dustups over the years. A Boston police officer was killed outside a few years back trying to break up a fight. The guys on the other side of us at the bar are huddled close together like they're hatching a scheme. I think I hear the phrase Russian mafia. Woops.

Time to stop eavesdropping.

I had ordered a couple beers and a bag of chips before, then left the change on the bar for a tip. When it's time for the second round the bartender pulls a few ones from the tip to pay for it. "No, that's for you," I say. I forget how things work in a lot of dives. At a place like this, the old timers line up their ones on the bar before they get started like a kid putting quarters up on the video game at an arcade. As they drink their way through the day the bartender usually just figures out the cost for them as they go, pulling bills off the pile as needed. Eventually they run out of lives and it's game over.

"There aren't too many bars like this around here any more?" I ask the bartender. "No. There's only two bars in town now. I mean, there are restaurants..." At one point Charlestown was in the Guinness Book of World Records for most bars per square mile, she says. Let's see, there was JJ McCarthy's, Monument Tavern, Blue Mirror, Horseshoe Tavern, Morning Glory , Gentleman Jim's, McAvoy's, The Cobblestone, Nat's, Gem Tavern, The Stork Club and The Woods Club to name but a fraction of long gone bars.

"I don't remember how many it was in Charlestown. Sixty eight bars? Now, there's... not. It's not like they all closed at once, it was just...over time, one by one. It's just hard to stay in business."

Tavern At the End of the World

108 Cambridge St., Charlestown
Phone: 617-241-4999

Dive Bar Rating

Living at the edge of a city's limits can be a problem for residents. Sanitation workers or plow drivers new on the job often don't realize streets there are actually on their route. The police might shrug off disturbances as falling outside of their jurisdiction. Tax assessors might jam you up good when your home splits zip codes. Your kids might be shut out of a preferred school systems. Or, if you're a bar, people might have no idea how to look up your location because they thought it was in a different city.

Turns out this divey little Irish pub in an area I'd always thought of as Somerville is actually in Charlestown. That sort of geographical confusion is where it takes its name from. In more ways than one, this area does feel like the end of the world. The sky is blotted out by the grim over hang of I-93, the Mystic River is northeast, a sinister industrial park sprawls outward to the south like some arch-villain's missile building complex. Sullivan Station, a major bus and Orange Line throughway is nearby. The iconic, defunct Schraft's candy factory is in the distance. Everything else there is to see is either a gas station or a package store or a pot hole. Welcome to Somerville. Or Charlestown, or whatever.

It could be worse. The spot that the Tavern occupies now used to be a notorious dive called the Town Line. "Oh it was brutal," Stevie, the curt Irish bar man tells me. People doing coke off the bar in the middle of the day out in the open, he says. "It's different now. Different clientele, different everything."

It is different. They've made significant strides toward turning the space into a respectable joint, and for the most part it's worked. Sorry to say, it's still a dive all the same. An impressive selection of microbrews and pub food, and a lineup of live music and comedy on the weekend can't erase five decades or so of decadence. The Tavern is yet another example of how the essence of a longstanding dive lingers long after a design overhaul. You can't remodel over a ghost. Better to nuke the site from orbit. It's the only way to be sure.

Stevie's a bit surly, but he's garrulous with the group of old regulars when I come in. There's a twentyish couple in black hoodies noshing on burgers at one of the tables in the small room. It is rather small in here in fact, coming across more like an old Massachusetts colonial residence where someone decided to put a bar up in their living room. It's like the Plymouth Plantation version of a dive bar, save for the retro movie posters and CD juke box on the wall (hipster alert: Tom Waits, The Kinks, Waylon Jennings alongside soul and British Invasion records). The old-seeming hard wood floors are new, as are the replica wooden period tables. The ceilings are low. I almost expected to see a butter churner in the corner.

"This is a dive," my girlfriend Michelle says. "It's in the architecture. They don't make places like this any more, even if it's new. The neighborhood helps too. It's just a minute away from the lot where your car usually gets towed to."

She's right. The Town Line, and the town line neighborhood, just feels like an area that knows where the bodies are buried so to speak. It's like when you move into an apartment where some dirt went down at some point. You know it. You feel it in your bones that the light switches and the door knobs have gone through a trauma. Still, the injection of youth here—beer snobs, music fans etc.—helps image-wise, but the Tavern is largely suspended in a transition between its past and future. It's like a dude in the middle of getting dressed when the fire alarm goes off, then has to run outside half naked.

(Dave Wedge)

DORCHESTER

Centre Bar

1664 Dorchester Ave., Dorchester
Phone: 617-436-0700

Dive Bar Rating

Heading south down the Ave. through always under-construction Field's Corner, toward this Irish immigrant pub, you'll pass by examples of the two extremes that Boston Irish dives have to look forward to in the near future. On one side there's the Blarney Stone, one of those mega-sports complex type Irish bars that are basically sports and booze theme parks for adults. On the other you've got the dearly departed dive the Emerald Isle, its name on the walls out front now faded almost away to nothing. You can either update into the new style, or you can pass away into history. The Centre Bar seems to be aiming to split the difference. It's actually not even that old, but the handsome pub affectations it wears are worn into what looks like decades of use.

The space here is also an example of the two ways you can go when you're opening an Irish pub. You can turn the dial too far in one direction and end up like a phoney tourist trap, or, more likely when you're in a neighborhood like this with tons of immigrants, you can maintain a scruffy, weathered charm. Centre Bar walks the line with its bright red walls, homey fireplace, and scuffed-up wooden floors. They've crammed every available inch of space with knick-knacks and curiosities, coats of arms, ship models, antique bar signs and weirdest of all, framed pictures of bad-ass cars taking sick jumps. Not sure what that has to do with Ireland, but I'm sure they know better than me. It doesn't hurt the Ireland-quotient when you're filled almost exclusively with clientele speaking in brogues, whether it's the working guys in all white painter's clothes, old timers in cute little drinking hats, beefy sports fans, or twentyish Irish girls in short skirts and reeking of perfume. And that's just on a random Wednesday at nine o'clock. On weekend nights it fills in even more with hood regulars who come for DJs and the occasional live act.

Much of the rest of the room were cheering on the Red Sox, despite the fact that they're long out of playoff contention by this point in September. It was sort of heartening to see. So that's what an actual, non-bandwagon sports fan looks like. At the bar there's another American guy arguing with the Irish one next to him over which country's football is more authentic. "In American football, you don't see the hit coming," he said. "But in rugby, you're getting hit all the time from all sides." It's a common argument in places like this. It really all balances out to the same thing in the end though, doesn't it? Same thing with both country's bars. You get hit, you fall down, and it isn't pretty. Then you get back up and try again. The dive bar extinction forces moving in from the city down the Ave., though? That's the type of opponent that's harder to put up a fight against. They'll certainly try over here.

High Traffic Bathroom Stalls

Hogan's Run

The Model Cafe

The Eagle

Old Sully's

Upstairs Downstairs

Parrotta's Alpine Lodge

BK's

Ace's High

Croke Park/ Whitey's

The Dot Tavern

840 Dorchester Ave., Dorchester
Phone:617-288-6288

Dive Bar Rating

A lot has been said over the years about the perils of high end clubs with velvet ropes and judgmental bouncers scoping out how nicely you're dressed while you stand in line waiting to pay fifty dollars for a drink. But at places like the Dot the exact opposite is true. Instead of an ex-college lineman with a clipboard there will usually be a team of old timers gunning butts outside throwing the stink eye at anyone who doesn't look like they were born, bred and sentenced to keel over at a barstool within a three block radius. Fortunately for me, there was a Bruins game on in the Dot on a quiet week night, so at least that provided me with a pretense for wandering in alone without knowing anyone. Not that there was really anything to worry about here. Basic bar rules apply pretty much across the board wherever you go. Keep to yourself, don't act like an asshole, and no one will bother you.

I slunk into the hard, cracked vinyl bench with my $4 Jim Beam and pressed up against a faux brick wall hoping I'd blend into the scenery. The crowd of locals watching the game, or arguing at one end of the bar basically ignored the carpetbagger. Although somehow I was still filled with the tingling sense I'd have whenever I used to get up to no good in my younger days and there would be police around. Here it was the same unease in reverse. I felt like I wasn't up to anything sketchy enough.

Any dive bar is going to have its inordinate share of drunk older men drinking at the bar. It's only in the real deal neighborhood spots like this where you'll find the female of the species. The accent here was a mix of working class Boston and Irish brogue, which is a truly musical artifact. It only reaches full power when shouted in furious voice, which you probably won't have to wait too long to hear at a place like the Dot when a hockey homer and his old lady start mixing it up. They should put that shrill cacophony in a museum.

After a bourbon I started to feel free to actually take my eyes off the game and drink in the full, divey bloom of the room. The bar area is long and thin, but there's a second room around the corner with foosball and pool and video games. The building is below a residence, but it's built thick and low to the ground, and aside from two tiny windows in front, it would make a great place to fortify yourselves against an outbreak of the zombie virus.

Before long my friend Dave Wedge showed up. He's a reporter for the *Boston Herald*, and he's lived in the area for a few years. Dorchester has had a pretty hearty resistance to complete gentrification, he says, unlike Southie or Chelsea. "Southie has this class war fueled by all the young kids that move in," he says. "The old school people don't like kids pissing on their doorstep at three in the morning. It's transient there. This neighborhood isn't like that. People buy houses here. It's still a predominantly blue collar neighborhood." There are housing projects, and a sober house nearby where he lives right around the corner, he says. "But there are lots of gay couples and young professional moving in across from Asian and black families as well." With that he ambles up to the bar to play a few Keno numbers. If he wants to show me the Dot dive bar experience, he's got to do it right.

(Dave Wedge)

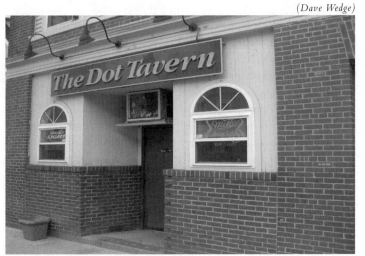

Dublin House

7 Stoughton St., Dorchester
Phone: 617-282-2235

Dive Bar Rating

Here's an image I never thought would come into my head as long as I lived: Imagine if legendary Celtics coach Red Auerbach retired early and decided to embark on a second career as a DJ spinning hip hop on Hot 97. What kind of bar do you think he'd hang out in? Check out Dublin House, aka Yaz's, and you've got your answer.

You can read the history of a changing Dorchester in the mashup of styles exhibited in this cavernous dive bar. Dorchester has long been one of the major centers for immigration in the city, particularly for the Irish, and it still is today. But this area, Upham's Corner, has become home to a huge Cape Verdean community in the past decade or so. The conflict, or rather the marriage of culture is played out quite literally inside here. It's an Irish bar by name and a sports bar by reputation ("Yaz" being the former Red Sox great Carl Yastrzemski), and a dive bar by appearance, but it's also a dance club by night that turns into one of the area's hottest, if a bit, how do you say, fighty, scenes. So that means you've got weathered wooden booths, walls cramped with sports memorabilia, dangling beer flags, old framed photos of iconic Boston figures, and fucked up tile floors like any other dive, but there's also a massive wall of speakers by a dance floor in the back half of the big room ready to blast your dome off and make you move your ass. The incongruity is almost vertigo-inducing. Today most of the patrons, and the staff, are black, but it's like they've simply adopted the old Irish bar that was standing there and said, "Yeah, this will do fine." Kind of awesome actually. You might call that a metaphor for Dorchester in general.

Because it's a popular dance spot in the center of Dorchester, there can be a dangerous vibe here at times. Signs posted on the walls alert patrons to the no weapons policy, which I happen to be a big fan of in any bar, and on weekends there is a police presence here. But the crowds, and the occasional knucklehead acting up are worth it, because the girls, and the music here, are popping off. Hip hop, merengue, reggaeton and dancehall nights, to name a few, are some of the weekly parties that go down. If that doesn't interest you, you can just come by earlier in the night, when it looks like any other average, run down Irish sports dive. The floors and the bar are sticky, the beers come in plastic cups and the food might be served on a styrofoam plate, but you'll be so busy trying to wrap your head around this awesome amalgamation of cultures that you won't have time to think about any of that. Who do you suppose Red's favorite rapper was, by the way? I'm guessing Biggie.

(Dave Wedge)

Interview with Dennis Lehane

Dorchester's Dennis Lehane, author of books like *Mystic River*, *Gone Baby Gone*, and *Shutter Island*, has built a brillitant career writing about the types of characters who inhabit Boston's seedier dive bars. I asked him about some of the bars he used as inspiration for setting in his Boston-based novels.

I feel like a lot of your characters hang out in dive bars.

Oh yeah, that would be a good description. But most of the actual dive bars I love are gone. I'm looking at an older Boston. Obviously The Rat. The Midnight Court. The Hammond was a great one with one of the best jukeboxes in the city, right out of Washington Square. That was a great one. The Cantab is still there in Central Square. Bunratty's. There was one, I think it was called Sullivan's although that's not really narrowing it down. There's Sullivan's in Charlestown, which I've spent some time at. It was in Union Square, two doors down from the Model.

O'Malley's. That's gone, they've turned it into like a hipster beer garden.

Oh no, really? It was owned by a guy, I assume he must have passed on by now. A guy named Red. He kept a map on the wall of the globe, and he had these pushpins on the map. When you went up and finally noticed and said 'What do these pushpins signify?' he'd say they were every single place he'd been in the world. He was a merchant marine.

And then if he really liked you he'd reach behind and pull out George Harrison's autobiography. He was mentioned in it because George Harrison dated his sister. Him and George Harrison went and got drunk in Germany back in the day. It was his big pride. He'd pull that out like it was the Bible. We were in there once and we said we heard this crazy rumor that he got robbed today. And he said 'I did.'

Then he pointed out the bullet hole. We were like 'You're opened for business?' He said 'They were punks.' I loved that place. Two kids came in and robbed him and he was like 'Fucking kids robbed me on a Saturday afternoon? There was no money!' But he stayed open. That was a great place.

What were some of your other favorites?

Way back in the day when it was a real brawlers bar we used to go to Midnight Court before it became Jose Mcintyre's. Just on that block of bars before you hit Faneuil Hall itself.

The funny thing about those bars is that there are more fights in them now than in most dive bars because of all the young kids.

There's a whole frat boy mentality about fighting now. These are the same fucking morons who turn over cars when we win the World Series. Back then it was known as a gun runner bar. They used to run guns for the IRA. They used to keep this hose behind the bar, literally, to hose off the blood. If you walked in the door and screamed 'INS!' they went out the windows like rats. This was the late eighties. We were doing social services work. It was the only place you could go in after a day of work. They had really cheap beer too.

What makes a dive bar a dive?

There has to be a difference between a dive bar and a skeevy bar. Like a skeevy bar you wouldn't go in with a woman on a bet. The Rat would scare off women, but if it didn't you knew she was cool. I used to blind date test people that way. I assume that's the reason I never got laid.

The difference between a dive bar and a skeevy bar is in a dive what you get is lack of pretension. You get a good solid bar that serves good drinks. But it's not doing anything else. It's not trying to serve you any sort of froufrou appetizers or a micro brew. It's got a pool table usually with a short stick half the time. It's got a really good music. A skeevy bar is just a dirty bar, where you don't feel safe and you certainly don't feel safe for your girlfriend. I would say that's the crucial difference.

I would say that's the job of your book, to really define the difference. Another one, used to be called the Lincoln, on that little stretch called Birmingham Parkway in Brighton. That one went through like nineteen different names. I remember when it was the Lincoln, for one year, it was a great dive. It would scare the shit out of a lot of people that walked in there, and you'd be like, 'No this is a dive, not a dangerous bar.' Then they did a couple of personnel changes and it became a dangerous bar over night. I stopped going there. I loved going when it was a good shit hole. Beyond that I wouldn't know how to define it. Except it's like pornography you kind of know it when you know it.

It seems like it's a lot less dangerous in general now at dive bars. I feel like now anywhere you go, you just walk in and drink your beer and mind your business and you'll be fine. But I get the impression that back in your day in South Boston or Dorchester you could walk into a place and it would be like the record scratching and everyone would look at you like who the fuck is this guy?

That would have been true back in the days of Triple O's and Streetlights. What you're seeing is the price of gentrification. If you went into Sully's or the Iron Horse in Charlestown, even when I moved back there in the early nineties, that was some rough trade. It was like don't fuck it up. And now... I just saw The Iron Horse today and it looks like The Kells.

I think what happened...there was one bar where I remember it was the end of Southie as we know it. The first of the nice Irish bars. It was called The Abbey. It was the first one where you were like, well someone put some real money into this bar. It was meant to look like Ireland, not like Irish America. That was the beginning, and then the trend just blew up across Southie. And now Southie is gone, it's gentrified. Every now and again you'll see it like on St Patrick's Day. The old Southie will come back if you hang out after the parade. You'll see these feral kids moving in packs ready to fuck you up because you're not from Southie.

What about Dorchester where a lot of your books are set?

I am very proprietary about Dorchester, so I don't want to speak about something I don't understand anymore. I don't drink on Dot Ave. anymore. All my friends left, my family left. I go back every now and then to see an old friend, but it's not like I'm hanging at the Banshee. The last time I was in Dot I was in Donovan's up in Savin Hill. This was five years ago.

I think most of these places if you go in and act like an asshole, then yeah, maybe... We were in some place in the North End last year, and my wife had some acquaintances with her, they weren't even friends. They started getting loud, and I was like, 'Do you guys understand what kind of bar you're in? I know it seems all cute and colorful to you, but you're in the middle of a Scorsese film.' You can still find those places. Certainly I think Tom English's in Dorchester, that was always known very much as a local bar. They had no desire to have outsiders come in. They weren't like, 'We have a great juke box, try our Guinness!'

So many places, like that one in particular, you look across the street and there are these new condos going up.

I do think the new gilded age isn't over. We're still in it. We thought it went with the stock market bust, but urban areas are just pricing out the cool people.

You mention a lot of bars in Darkness, Take My Hand. TT the Bear's, Harper's Ferry. You must have been a big rock and roll fan.

Oh yeah. Harper's was great because they'd get these great unheard of blues acts in there. The other connection you'll find in almost every bar I liked was a pool table. We used to call it the Mo-del. They had the most infamous short stick. The worst fucking angle on a pool table. It was like shooting pool in your friend's small closet. But it was great. You could tell guys who were shooting there forever by the way they handled that short stick. The Rat used to have great pool tables upstairs. That was my big thing, pool tables and juke boxes.

The art of the jukebox is dead now with all the internet juke boxes. There's something to be said for a limited selection.

You knew the taste of the bar owner, and it was really cool. It was like, wow, this guy is into things nobody has ever heard of except for us hipsters. And it was really cool. It's the problem with an iPod, when do you sit and listen to a full CD anymore?

What does your fictional Black Emerald bar look like?

It's what the Banshee used to be. Before the Banshee it was called Bonds. It was a straight up dive bar. They nailed it on the original hard cover of that book. It amazed me. I said this is the bar. You walked in and there was just a bar to the left. Tight squeeze, a rubber tile floor, a bunch of bar stools. A bar rack on the wall to the right. It just went straight back like a shot gun bar. Man, that was a dive. It was beyond a dive, it was a scary place. I think that's where I got the idea. Now the Banshee is beautiful. It's got Irish breakfast on Sunday.

Is that where you got the idea for the underworld stuff?

Yeah there was that. My dad was taking me to bars since I was nine years old. He's supposed to be at the farmer's market. He'd buy all the vegetables in five minutes then we'd go to Pete and Dick's on Dot Ave.

There's a quote in *Shutter Island* **that I think sums up what I'm thinking about in terms of gentrification of the city: "What do you lose when you sweep a floor, Teddy? Dust. Crumbs that would otherwise draw ants. But what of the earring she misplaced? Is that in the trash now too?"**

Without a doubt that's originally what that line applied to. I originally came up with that image when I was thinking about *Mystic River*. I even wrote in an op ed in the Globe in a piece about gentrification, I said what do you lose when you sweep the floor?

I don't want to romanticize the old Boston by any means. There was a lot of it that was grungy and racist and violently provincial. And there's nothing good to be said about that. But at the same time, the note I had when I was writing *Mystic River* and I was living in Charlestown was I said 'What happens when Pat's Pizza becomes a Starbucks?' And that's what happened. It's not so much gentrification, it's globalization, and it's just killing character man, it's wiping it out. I wish I could put a positive spin on it, it's great for crime rates and all. You see that this is going on in urban areas all over the country and it's really depressing. I came back here last night and I was looking out at the city thinking about how much of my life has been fashioned by nights running through this city. We all lived downtown and we were poor as shit. I just don't think that's possible now.

The Eire Pub

795 Adams St., Dorchester
Phone: 617-436-0088

Dive Bar Rating

Because of its iconic status as an Irish Catholic Boston working-man's type pub, it's become standard for campaigning Massachusetts politicians to stop in here and show off their blue-collar cred, or in some cases, the lack thereof. But the big national names have come in over the years as well. Ronald Reagan passed through in 1983 and wowed the crowds by spending time talking to everyone and generally not seeming like a robotic evil overlord for five minutes. In 1992 Bill Clinton hammed it up himself over a few pints with the lads. Those aren't exactly your every day Eire drinkers, mind you, but it's something that the pub is proud of, and framed photos and newspaper clippings around the large, hall-sized tavern dominated by a horseshoe-shaped bar are left up as reminders of the good old days. You know, like when presidential candidates actually paid attention to Massachusetts.

Or were they that good? Maybe not if you were a woman. The large marquee out front has the words "Men's Bar" stamped on either side twice. A second sign calls the Eire a "gentlemen's prestige bar." Refusing to serve women would be illegal now of course, but it wasn't so long ago that in many bars throughout the city women literally weren't allowed to come in. Which brings up a number of thorny issues, not least of which is where the hell did you go back then to pick up chicks?

"Though it's called a gentleman's bar, women are allowed in," *Boston Phoenix* reporter Chris Faraone tells me. "But though women are allowed in, there's no doubt that it is indeed a gentleman's bar."

My friend Sarah who used to drink in this neighborhood a lot agrees. She says she always felt the strange men's club thing going on in here. "I definitely never felt like it was actually cool for me to be in the Eire. I guess that's the prevalent sensation I am left with after venturing into any kind of ancient watering hole. I felt like the bar was holding its breath during my short visits."

There were a few women in here when I came in last however, but I can see what they're saying. The gentlemen in question here tend to be union workers and a large number of freshly arrived Irish immigrants who seem to be shipped in daily to this part of Dorchester. Even the pizza place next door to the bar here is Irish. (The Chinese place is still Chinese though, as far as I can tell.) Bars like this are like an auxiliary to the immigration offices, or a gateway easing the newly arrived on their transition from Ireland to Boston.

The men folk are here for a lot of reasons; maybe it is to get away from the wife for a while. Or maybe it's for the chalkboard specials like pastrami sandwiches for $4.50 and hot dogs for a $1, or because the bartenders, with a sort of rumpled professionalism in their white shirts and vests have their beer in front of the regulars before they've had a chance to fully sit down. For a taste of how Boston used to be, for better or worse, you couldn't ask for much more. Except for maybe a few pretty faces to look at.

(Dave Wedge)

Lower Mills Pub

2269 Dorchester Ave., Dorchester
No phone

Dive Bar Rating

🍾🍾🍾🍾🍾

This Lower Mills neighborhood of Dorchester is starting to feel the gravitational pull of nearby Milton Village. Coming along with that has been a bevy of apartment and condo developments, new businesses moving in, cafes, antique shops and so on. It's less crowded than other parts of Dorchester, with fewer multi-family homes, and also relatively leafy; you could almost convince yourself you were in the suburbs if you looked at it just right. But easy T access to the city, and the fact that you can walk to most places over here keep it situated in the urban. Add all of those things together and you get a recipe for disaster for dive bars like this one.

"I can't believe this place still exists," Paul, a drinker I meet at the bar here tells me. He grew up in the neighborhood, and has just returned after moving away for years. He used to be able to walk up and down the Ave. when he was eighteen, stopping at dozens of bars on the way to the city. Most of those are gone now, he says. Now the place next door is called Ledge. It's a sleek, modern restaurant that serves flatbreads and arancinis and fancy pasta dishes. Next to that is Yerbe Mate, an organic tea shop for hippies I guess, and the Common Ground Cafe, a yuppie coffee store. "That place the Ledge, we used to call it the wax museum," Paul says of its previous incarnation. "You'd walk in and see the same guys sitting there, looking like they hadn't moved."

That might usually apply to the gang at the Lower Mills tonight, but they're exceptionally animated, riled up by the football game on the small TVs over the bar. I'm pretty excited too, I have to say, but more so about my drink. The whiskey I've just been served by Larry the bartender, a no-nonsense type of guy who seems slightly ashamed by the tenor of his wasted patrons tonight, may be the tallest pour of whiskey I've ever been served. It's nearly overflowing.

"That place is out of my range," Rene tells me, when I ask him if he's been over to Ledge yet. He's lived across the street for twenty years. Another regular in an over-sized suit, like David Byrne in Talking Heads big, is walking down the length of the bar like a shit-faced politician who just lost the election, glad-handing everyone sarcastically. "Jerry, good to see you. Sean, I never liked you." When he gets to me he pauses for a second, trying to figure out what to do. "You. I don't know you. But have a good night anyway."

Yeah, it's that type of place. The bar is an old, fortress-like little room, all beaten up wood, formica, and painted brick walls. One of the walls is covered in a giant Quaker Oats mural. It feels old in here, but not the usual dive-bar old. The low ceilings are crossed by ancient looking wooden beams that hint at the type of Revolutionary era architecture that you can still find in pockets around here.

Rene used to play on a softball team for a bar around the corner called Eddy's. It's long gone by now. There were ten teams coming out of that one bar, he says, which is a point of pride for him still. Back inside he wants to buy me a beer, but everyone is getting a little woozy in here, and no one is making sense anymore. People are mumbling to themselves, and walking funny when they get up to use the bathroom. I think I've had my fill of drunken exclamations for the night. Instead I head next door to Ledge where I can hang out with thirty-somethings in tucked-in shirts eating tomato salads while the football game flickers above us, unwatched.

Peggy O'Neil's

1310 Dorchester Ave., Dorchester
Phone: 617-265-9236

Dive Bar Rating

There is a such a confluence of bar styles at work here it's a good example of the neighborhood bar that retains its early evening and daytime presence while also serving as a boozy playground for area twenty-somethings by night. Lots of old hood bars still have their disused kitchenette set up behind the bar, but there aren't many where you'll see the old lady barkeep using it at 9 pm on a Wednesday night grilling up subs and bringing steaming plates of lasagna down to the guys scratching away at their lottery tickets and drinking bottled beer out of 8 oz glasses. This is the first time I've ever actually thought about eating at one of these places.

On the other end of the spectrum, Peggy's has a cover charge on weekends, and it gets packed with Dot locals fired up on hormones and looking for beef. "That place is full of girl fights and asbestos," one friend told me. "It is a virtual Dot whore-a-thon on weekends," another said. "A good place to pick up a MILF in her early 20s. If her boyfriend isn't out on parole."

I don't happen to be in the market for any of that, not now anyway, but for a quiet spot to nurse a pint on a weeknight it's pretty ideal. There's a big back room with nice couches and pool tables, but out front at the bar dive cliches abound. It's dim in here, the tiny windows of the sturdy brick edifice are covered by homey curtains, pool trophies are on display near the Captain Morgan's shot chiller machine, and old dudes with Boston politician style white hair helmets are face deep in their bowls of loud mouth soup. Next to them there's a kid in biker attire with tats and one of those choo choo train hats though. Both types.

I've often said that once an old local haunt starts to put money back into itself after it's become accustomed to drawing a big crowd of kids at night, it usually means it changes beyond repair. But that's not the case here, it's a peaceful coexistence. It's party DJs and shooters on one side, serious, business-like drinking on the other. Some people drink because it's fun, some people drink like it's a job. Some bars let you do both. Around here I think that passes for diversity.

Sonny's Adams Village Restaurant and Lounge

750 Adams St., Dorchester
Phone: 617-436-9432

Dive Bar Rating

In contrast to some of the other bars in the area where you'll find the actual criminals and parolees drinking, this neighborhood restaurant and bar is where their parents come to commiserate about their no-good kids while trying to enjoy a veal parmesan. For anyone who falls outside of that demo, it's also a reasonable place to have a low key pint or two and watch the game, or snack on the surprisingly decent pizza. The early bird specials prominently displayed throughout kind of give away the clientele's real age group though. Maybe that's because it's remained a family institution for so long. Sonny Elia opened the place in 1968, and his sons and grandsons took the ball and ran with it after he stepped down. They've made improvements in recent years, remodeling the place and installing a polished nautical theme, paying proper homage to the city's sports demi-gods, and updating the menu, but there's an actual cigarette machine up front next to the scratch ticket machine, let's not get ahead of ourselves here.

Still, you'd think that a place like this would be more lively and less downtrodden because it's also an actual restaurant where people from the area come to eat. But it somehow makes it so much worse to see families and old marrieds trying to have dinner ten feet from a police lineup of Keno addicts and booze hounds. Interestingly, this is almost the exact same layout as the Newtowne Grill over in Porter Square, a Cambridge dive bar/ family restaurant. But even though Adams Village and Porter are a long way apart in terms of miles and neighborhood makeup, it shows how dives are basically the same thing wherever you go.

I'm thinking about that when an old guy pulls up next to me at the bar. He's just come from home where six city cops paid a social call to his son. What were they looking for? Well they had a dog along for the ride too. He came to the only place he could think of after. It's actually heartbreaking to listen to him telling his story to the familiar regulars and the bartender who obviously know him well. But at least he has a place like this to go.

Tom English Bar

957 Dorchester Ave., Dorchester
Phone: 617-288-7748

This is the third spot my friend Dave and I have hit on Dorchester Ave. this week, and it's a lot different than he remembers from his last visit. "When I first went here this place was a dump, all formica. Now it's like the definition of putting lipstick on a pig." The old bar served as a model for Denis Lehane when he was writing the Dorchester-set "Gone Baby Gone." If you hadn't been in before you probably wouldn't even realize it had undergone a proper spiffying up. This bar, like Tom English's Cottage in Southie, gets its name from the man who founded it. Both remain in the family.

The renovations are so quaint they're almost tragic. But it's a nice hardwood bar, smooth and shining like the wood of a bowling alley lane—you might actually be able to pull off that old trick you only see in movies where the bartender slides a pint from one end to the other.

High top tables scattered throughout provide ample room to stake your claim on a seat while a rock band warms up in the corner. A lineup up of old timers are leaning heavily on the bar, all jutting elbow angles, guarded in the classic slumping dive-man's pose. They hold their drinks close in the crook of the arm, like a running back protecting the football. The last thing a professional athlete, or drinker for that matter, wants to do is fumble.

Jackie's on the bar tonight. She's a girl of about twenty two who's lived here in the neighborhood her entire life, and she's what Dave and I have decided is a perfect example of what you might call dive hot. It's the phenomenon where the very predictable lack of women in any scenario—a seafaring vessel, say, or an all male boarding school or a race car driver or a vice presidential candidate or the crew of spaceship or whatever—automatically turns any woman in the vicinity into the object of male affection.

"This is still a mostly neighborhood crowd," she tells us. "Even on the weekends there aren't ever really many young people in here." Jackie and her friends prefer Peggy O'Neil's down the street.

There are, however, $2.50 PBR drafts. The first one tastes and smells like piss, but the second one is the nectar of the gods. The charm of the setting adds to the beer's medicinal effects. It's 10 pm on a week night, I'm telling my life story to a guy I barely know, a townie cover band is playing "Don't Let Me Down", my favorite Beatles song, and I'm awkwardly failing to flirt with a girl with a wicked Boston accent and a nose ring. Doesn't get any better than that.

Dave wanders off to shoot pool with a little neighborhood guy who hops around the room like a coked up sprite. I watch from the bar while he pulls off a victory or two. "This guy smells like crack," he says. "You've entered into a whole other realm my friend."

I step outside for a smoke and consider the half million dollar condos across the street. A poorly timed development considering the economy, as most of them sit uninhabited and empty. The bar isn't empty though. Dives may be huge underdogs in a game versus yuppies and an omnivorous gentrification onslaught, but every now and again the little guy pulls off an upset.

(Dave Wedge)

Twelve Bens

315 Adams St., Dorchester
No Phone

Dive Bar Rating

The last few years have been tough times for dive bar owners throughout the city, but even more so for Dorchester in particular. The rapidly gentrifying blocks of Boston's biggest, but still largely blue collar neighborhood has made keeping up with the changes hard. Dorchester Ave. has been redeveloped the most, but it's crossed over gradually to nearby Adams St. somewhat too, where you'll find this sturdy Irish immigrant outpost. The long commercial thoroughfare still has its share of seedier bodegas and hole in the wall restaurants, and yes, plenty of dives, but they're being elbowed out by newer, more upscale eateries catering to the migrating professional class and young city-dwellers staking out new areas to populate. An influx of new ethnic populations has altered the predominately Irish makeup of the Ave. as well. A faltering economy and massive unemployment in Ireland, not to mention a poor economy here, have hindered the free movement of Irish emigrants to this part of the city in recent years.

That places like this still exist is a miracle. All this real estate can't be held onto by relatively unprofitable bars where regulars can spend $2-3 dollars on a pint. "Location cannibalism seems to be the m.o. of humanity," a friend who lives nearby says. "But sometimes places should be left alone to continue the service they provide. For example, I can't imagine the woman with the oxygen tanks, wheel chair, scratch tickets, and Newport Lights could smoke and scratch and watch Monday Night Football at some of the newer, improved bars while shooting the shit with her friends."

That's a good thing when it comes to finding real deal dive bars. Whether or not it's good for property values I'll leave for the homeowners in the area to fight out among themselves. For many bar owners, the temptation to sell their liquor license, which can often fetch up to $250,000, is too much.

If you come by Twelve Ben's pub though, you might not realize anything is changing at all. I talk a lot about how you can tell how authentic an Irish dive bar is based on the accents you hear at the bar, and while there are quite a few that fit the mold, they've got nothing on this place. In this unremarkable looking neighborhood pub with its drop tile ceilings, red paint job, tile floors and a bright wooden bar, I'd be surprised to even hear a Boston accent. In keeping with that, there are big photos of local rugby and gaelic football teams on the walls alongside Irish boxers.

On a recent Thursday night Irish twenty somethings are flirting and fucking around in front of a soccer match. The older lads are playing cards at the bar. There's a function room out back with steam trays laid out by the Buckhunter machine like they just had a catered party in here. In fact this is where a lot of the local families might hold the parties after Christenings and funerals and the like. The pressures of encroaching gentrification don't seem to have seeped into the cracks here just yet, and isn't that what a good dive bar is for after all? To make you forget, if just for a little while, the pressures of the world?

(Dave Wedge)

Upstairs Downstairs

469 Neponset Ave., Dorchester
Phone: 617-436-9589

🍾🍾🍾🍾🍾

This rough and rugged dive bar, wedged between a highway on ramp and a desolate few blocks of auto repair shops, and near one of Quinchester's (where Dorchester meets Quincy's) purgatory-like traffic circles, looks like a bowling alley with its colorfully playful sign. Inside runs with that theme as well, with video games, dartboards, posters of athletes covering the walls and other arcade-like fixtures. This sort of décor plays up the idea of how a lot of dive bars, even the ones where you'll find mostly older men, are really just examples of suspended adolescence at work. No surprise then that you'll often find drinkers in dives reverting to their childish states: yelling, drooling, nodding off for a nap, fighting when they don't get their way.

Speaking of fighting, Ups N Downs, as it's called, has a pretty menacing reputation in that regard. Fights over the past few years have placed the bar's liquor license in jeopardy, and plenty of people in the hospital on numerous occasions. On a recent Christmas a massive brawl in the bar spilled out onto the streets when a woman smashed one of the bartenders in the face with a bottle. This being Dorchester, he punched her right back in the fucking face. Every police car in the area was needed to control the situation. During another brawl one of the customers jumped behind the bar and emptied the cash register, while others made off with armfuls of liquor bottles out the back door. There are police officers on duty now on weekend nights in the bar's upstairs area.

That upstairs downstairs demarcation is where things get a little interesting here, if by interesting you mean racially fucked up. The name of the place implies a sort of segregation. Upstairs is for hip hop, downstairs is for Sinatra. Or to put it another way, upstairs is for blacks, downstairs is for whites. It's the same old shitty story of Dorchester race relations played out literally every night in the place people in the neighborhood go to get drunk. Like that's not asking for trouble. The bar, formerly known as the Pony Room, has been in operation for about 50 years.

Everyone seems friendly enough on the surface when I come on an early weeknight. The bartender is cute in that trashy Dorchester way, with tattoos on her neck and feet. I'm drinking with a few old guys watching the game and a seemingly reasonable guy in a Brett Favre jersey next to me. So what's upstairs like tonight? I want to know.

"You don't want to go up there," the bartender tells me.

"It's like cockroaches up there," the Favre fan says. "It's fucking awful. It's all black upstairs and all whites downstairs. Now you can't have glasses to drink out of up there anymore."

"It didn't used to be like that, but then they started playing the hip hop."

Wait a second, is this a joke? This is a joke right? I mean, I know Boston has a reputation, but we're in public here people. Instead I keep my mouth shut and my head down, because I'm a pussy. And what am I going to do, give a lecture?

"Ah well, as the world turns," the bartender says."

"As the neighborhood turns," another guy adds from across the bar. Then we all go back to staring at the Red Sox game, cheering on our racially diverse hometown heroes.

They Aren't All Irish Bars

You can't puke Magners out your nose around here without splashing it all over the bright red walls of some faux Irish pub or another. That's because—and don't quote me on this —I'm pretty sure there are more Irish people in Boston than in all of Ireland. That means every day is like St. Patrick's Day here, which is great because it combines three cool ideas: religion, national pride, and drinking like a homeless street fighter.

Anchovies

Deluxe Cafe

Shangrilla Chinese Restaurant

Wally's Cafe

Portugalia

Riverside Pizza

El Mondonguito

Pat "Packy" Connors Tavern

Taverna Medallo

Fasika

EAST BOSTON/CHELSEA

Chelsea Walk Pub

416 Broadway, Chelsea
Phone: 617-884-0146

Dive Bar Rating

Chelsea is a city unto itself, literally and figuratively, just across the Mystic River from Boston. It's notable for a few things: the historic brick buildings, its relative proximity to the city, and lower real estate prices which have made it an attractive alternative for artists and the gay population who are usually the trailblazers for seeking out new territory in the metro area. It's also home to one of the highest percentage Latino populations in greater Boston. The Bellingham Square area where you'll find this classic dive bar leans more toward the latter group, although it's got its fair share of African American drunks, white drunks, and every other type of drunk you can think of.

The block the bar sits on is a time capsule of turn of the century buildings and fifties era development. In fact aside from a few minor details —say, menacing gangs of kids circling around on bikes with bike cops following close behind—you can pretty much imagine it exactly as it was decades ago. Most of the shop fronts remain unchanged: old pharmacies, laundries and restaurants whose facades haven't changed since they were put up. There probably weren't this many liquor stores and check cashing places back in the day though. Likewise, the interior of the Chelsea Walk is out of its own time. It's a thin space, taken up mostly on one side by a long bar. It looks sort of like the mess deck of a seagoing vessel. More than a few of the drinkers in here seem to have long ago lost their sea legs. The walls are covered in wood panelling, boat wheels, harpoons, and port hole mirrors. Chelsea was historically an important seaside district during the early settling period of Boston and up into the last century.

Otherwise, it's a dive bar like any other. The bar top is covered in smooth tile that looks like it belongs on a bathroom floor, which is convenient if you have too many and need to rest your head on the bar. The gang in here has probably spent more than a few nights clinging for dear life to their own bathroom floor tiles at home. The racially diverse crowd is mostly indifferent to interlopers, although occasionally you might find your mettle being tested by a few close-walking brush-bys. In a bar like this, where locals can occasionally be territorial, that's a way of sniffing out a newcomer; it's like a shark bumping its nose up against the bottom of a boat to see what it's made of, whether or not it would make a good snack. The African American grandmother types you'll find decked out in leopard print jackets are a bit more welcoming. Maybe too much so. At least they're friendly, or misguided enough to eye me up as a different type of meat than the tough guys. It's a pleasant alternative to a lot of the other women you might see wandering down the street here on a sketchy weekend night. Many of them have the glazed over, shambling walk of a horde of bored zombies. Then again, if the bar in my neighborhood sold $1.50 drafts, I might end up developing a bit of walking problem myself.

Best dives for playing games

The Last Drop

Silhouette Lounge

Beacon Hill Pub

Punter's Pub

Sullivan's Tap

The Courtside Restaurant and Pub

Twelve Bens

The Drinking Fountain

On the Hill Tavern

The Shannon Tavern

Eddie C's

34 Maverick Square, East Boston
Phone: 617-567-9395

Dive Bar Rating

It's a cliché to refer to a dive bar as being like the cantina from *Star Wars,* but honestly, that's the scene that was playing on the television when I wandered into Eddie C's on a stifling Saturday evening, so my hand is forced here. The crowd isn't quite that space-drunk and rambunctious in here, but it's almost as diverse: black dudes, Colombians, old Italians, a five hundred year old dressed up as a kid's Halloween costume version of a hobo. Actually, check that, that's his real outfit. No aliens or Jedis in sight, but give it time, the rush hasn't started yet.

A smattering of younger neighborhood professionals, part of the newer influx into Maverick Square, Eastie's busiest commercial district, whet their thirst here as well. They don't have much of a choice. Aside from dive bars and the dozens of restaurants catering to the Latino population, there aren't too many other options in terms of nightlife over here yet. But since Maverick is a major bus and T transit area, there are always people on the move. A bar like this has to cater to all types. Hopefully everyone likes the current motif, which you might describe as the basement dungeon of a New York sports fan. Curiously the bar seems to have a thing for the Yankees, and Babe Ruth in particular. How does a bar in Boston put up with that? I know Ruth played for the Sox back when, but come on. All of these pictures should have been torn down in a fit of crowd-think homer rage like a scene out of "Day of the Locusts" years ago. Although a Bill Simmons ESPN column from a while back told a story about a group of Sox yahoos tying a Yankees fan up to a tree outside the bar here, so maybe I just came on the wrong night. I also heard a story about a woman taking a chunk out of another woman's face during a bar brawl at Eddie C's. Han Solo shooting a dude under the table sort of pales in comparison to that.

Speaking of *Star Wars*, there are dozens of festive paper stars hanging from the ceiling, but they aren't exactly lightening the mood. It's dark in here. Dark and sort of dank. It feels like a long time ago in galaxy far away. The green linoleum tile floors are beat up and the booths are all weathered wood. The bathroom looks like a haunted mine shaft.

I asked my man Mike who lives in Eastie what the deal is with Eddie C's. Predictably, he mentioned the *Star Wars* analogy. "It's a bit weird, similar to the bar on Tatooine in *Star Wars*." Last time he was in he says "there were a lot of guys dressed in drag. As much as it was interesting, it was also a bit strange because during the day it seems to be kind of normal and everyone is pretty straight-laced. But when the sun goes down it turns into a sight."

Right now it's a happy medium. The bartender is a nice older woman dressed as if she's twenty years younger than she really is. She's apparently never seen *Star Wars* before. I tell her this is the version where George Lucas went back and "improved upon" the original, inserting all sorts of extra crap that no one asked for and no one needed. Bars like this are a reminder that some things are just impossible to fix. And why would you want to?

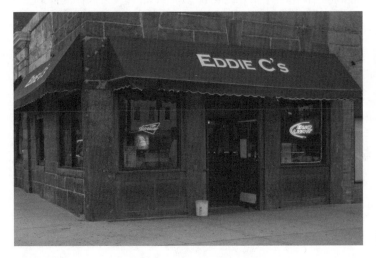

Parrotta's Alpine Lodge

77 Winnisimmet St., Chelsea
No phone

It's not hard to imagine why the former Boston outpost of Chelsea has become an attractive option for the colonizing hoards fleeing renters' persecution in some perverted analogy of the city's original settlers. A straight shot down the brick and stone road on which this classic dive sits there's the type of gorgeous view of the city skyline that people pay a million dollars to wake up to every day. Even so, the neighborhood Parrotta's is in still isn't much to look at—here's a yuppie walking a couple of her purebred dogs down an unlit street when I pull in, which either says a lot about the lack of nighttime skullduggery over here or else her faith in her cute little dogs' ferocity. But when you're standing in a pile of shit looking up at a beautiful sunrise, it's still nice to feel the distant glow, right?

Speaking of a pile of shit, the bar here is straight from the long-ago-broken townie dive mold. There's an old box phone booth, an ancient sixties era cartoon framed on the wall illustrating the finer points of operating with beer goggles (I'd have to have a thousand beers first for those to kick in for me here), and a mysterious back room with loud grunts coming from it sporadically. It's actually another bar room that used to be called Old Pal's Piano Lounge; only the first two words of that title seem to have any relevance anymore. There's a formica bar top, tile and plywood walls, and bar seats held together with duct tape. This whole place feels like it's held together with duct tape, and so do I after a couple of plastic cups full of whiskey. When I'm trying to find the bathroom later I feel like a cannibal family has my friends on meathooks in the basement and I'm trying to escape to get help. I don't think I'd make it out. It smells like refrigerated must balls in here.

The bartender isn't doing much actual tending of, you know, the bar, but the regulars seem to be cruising on auto-pilot anyway. She's got the miserable, approaching-sociopathic disinterest of a Tobin Bridge toll collector; she's seen everyone pass through, in other words. There's a ten thousand year old man in a Red Sox wind breaker sitting backwards at the bar next to me. He doesn't move for two hours, or respond to my efforts toward conversation. The rest of the crowd down the bar is zipping around on fast-forward. It doesn't seem like there's much room for the middle ground in here. It's a ship of doomed souls, I think, considering the large boat wheel hung over bar. I feel like I could reach out and grab it and steer the whole place down the hill into the river and set sail.

Taverna Medallo

411 Chelsea St., East Boston
Phone: 617-567-2727

Dive Bar Rating

Unlike every other square inch of the city, East Boston has been a little slower on the gentrification uptake. That's partly because you have to take an underground space tunnel to get here from the city proper, and partly because of the constant overhead thunder rattle of planes coming and going from nearby Logan Airport. It may offer stunning views of the skyline and have beautiful harbor-side landscapes outside of the commercial areas, but no one wants to live under an airport. As a result, or maybe it's the other way around actually, it's always been a prime settling area for immigrants to the city. At times that's meant a heavy influx of either Irish or Italians, but in the past decade it's become a predominantly Latino neighborhood. There are plenty of areas where you can feel like you've stumbled through a wormhole into downtown Bogota, (or Port-au-Prince, or Hanoi) which is cool in terms of diversity, and for knife-fighting enthusiasts, but also great if you're ever planning on scaring the shit out of your racist Republican dad on a trip to the city.

Like a lot of primarily immigrant bars, Medallo falls into a hard to define dive category. Is it a dive? Well....you ever have a hard time figuring out if a dude was gay or just foreign? Same thing here. It's also so dark in here I honestly couldn't really say what it looks like. Yellow...maybe? I think that glowing thing over there is a light... of some sort? There are a few Spanish speaking guys holding court by the front window when I walk in. The blinds are drawn and the briefest hint of the fading light outside is curling through the cracks.

The bartender, a beautiful Colombian woman, is pleasant, but obviously surprised by my arrival. After serving me my beer she retreats to the stereo to crank up the already deafening Spanish pop ballads. Gringo test of some sort perhaps? I tough it out, but I don't think I'll ever hear out of my left ear again. (I am dedicated to my work.) I consider trying out some of my awesome kitchen Spanish on her, but think better of it. It's not so much that I don't feel welcome, it's more like I've wandered into a party I wasn't invited to and the hosts are too polite to come right out and ask me to leave.

Taverna Medallo

At night the Medallo turns into a thriving nightclub, but by day it's got all the tell tale dive signifiers. Quiet men drinking quietly, insulated from the world by a darkness broken only by the glare of the boring, monotonous television; Spanish language informercials to be precise. Turns out they sell the same useless shit on those too. Like a lot of other bars they're just making an effort to recapture a little bit of the familiar in an unfamiliar place. Usually in Boston that means leaning toward some watered-down Irish-ness. Not to sound like a liberal arts school brochure here, but anytime you can add an extra touch of diversity to your regular routine it helps you see the world in a slightly different way.

OK, just kidding. This is the same old product as anywhere else but in a slightly different wrapper. All the same I kind of love this place, even if it scares me a little. I don't want to really go to a bar that's too excited to have me there anyway.

Trainor's Cafe

127 Maverick St., East Boston
Phone: 617-567-6995

Dive Bar Rating

Across the street from this old Italian dive there's a thematically convenient bodega called Los Paisano's. So that's your cultural story of Eastie in a nutshell. In the bar the Italian side of the family is representing well, but it's polyglot. Down the bar dos borachos are arguing en Espanol while a Vietnamese guy is arguing with himself. The paisanos are leaning into a hard day's relaxing, enjoying an afternoon glass of vino.

It's a wide open space in here, with doors open at both ends, so there's plenty of room for the varied trade winds to blow wherever they may. I'm at the beat up wooden bar trying to figure out what the hell is going on with the music in here. A middle aged Italian dude in a track suit just put "True Blue" by Madonna on the juke. Everyone is into it. Maybe it's a Catholic thing? "You're never too young!" his buddy yells from across the room, which, although it doesn't make any sense, sort of describes the situation perfectly. The bartender pulls a fist full of cash from the register and sends the guy around the corner to the laundromat to make some change. Riiiight.

There are green and red neon lights spanning the length of the wall behind the bar. A surprising number of fish mounted on the walls too. Further up are a series of old ghostly, washed-out photos of Eastie of yore. They show tree-lined squares and old trolley cars. It's almost enough to send me off on a flight of historic fantasy, but the Madonna paradox is taking up all the space in my brain. These are tough guys. There's a damned telephone booth that you can sit in and close the door here. Who knows what kind of calls might have been made from that very spot near where the Scorsese rejects are old-man-grooving. "It's My Life" by Talk Talk comes on next. Ho-lee shit. Who knew Italian dives in East Boston were the hot spot for new wave dancing now?

Next to me a guy in a deeply-open-collar linen button down and linen pants, a pinkie ring and a smooth shit-eating grin is leaning against the bar . He's either a cheap mob villain wannabe or the most powerful coke dealer in the neighborhood. His girlfriend or niece or

EAST BOSTON/CHELSEA

BOSTON'S BEST DIVE BARS

whatever comes running in bouffant-first in a halo of hairspray. I can smell her before my eyeballs even register her presence. She pulls up to the bar way too close for my comfort. I don't know much, but I'm certain you don't get near a guy with a pinkie ring's girlfriend at a bar. Her friend is too young though. Like real young. The bar man asks her them to leave. "Be careful," Donnie Brasco over here tells them. "Both of you."

Victory Pub

1004 Bennington St., East Boston
Phone: 617-567-9242

Located in the hilly, waterside Orient Heights, a one time heavy Catholic Italian enclave, the Victory is at the intersection of hard urbanity and natural beauty. Just around the corner are the relative charms of Revere Beach (where you'll find plenty more dives I haven't covered here) and the gorgeous Belle Isle Marsh reservation area. This classic dive pub sits on a busy intersection at the north end of Eastie. Upstairs is a popular neighborhood restaurant called Top of the Pub, but the real action takes place in the street level bar. By action I mean shit show. Since nearby Revere has early closing times, everyone runs over here afterwards for their 2 am last call. That means it gets crowded late at night with people from Revere, which is basically like Boston's version of The Jersey Shore.

"It's a mix in here," the bartender says. "We get 21+ all the way up to a guy we've got who's 75 that comes in all the time. We get all the ethnics too. Brazilians, Mexicans, Puerto Ricans... We used to have a couple Moroccans in here but we got them out of here." Oh. Good?

It's about to get really busy she tells me. She's friendly and calls me hon about five more times than you'd expect over the course of a thirty second conversation, but she also looks to be about 185 pounds of solid muscle. Her boyfriend is coming in soon to work the door. "Otherwise I would knock somebody out," she says. I believe her.

The setup inside the bar should be familiar to anyone who's ever written a book about one hundred damn dive bars. They've got an impressive array of TVs in here, both new and old, Keno, a jukebox, video games, scratch tickets, bla bla bla. There are more than a few signs pointing out that they do not offer credit here. Wait, is that actually even a thing? Like people come in and ask for a beer then say they'll pay another time? What is this Bedford Falls? I guess if you've been coming to the same bar every day for your entire life you start to feel entitled, start to feel like you own the place.

Like any other dive worth going to it's all about the characters you'll meet inside. Simultaneously consuming an alcoholic beverage in the same vicinity as someone else levels the playing field. There's nowhere else besides a dive bar where you would find it normal to talk to a wasted guy without many teeth while his arms are loaded up with cuts of meat. Unless you work at a butcher shop with really lax safety standards.

I'm drinking a beer out of a brightly colored plastic cup when just such a man wanders in on his way back from the market. He's excited about his purchases. Everyone else seems to be too. Ribs, sirloin, peppers. This guy is all set up. Had to stop in here for a quick one before taking it home though. That's dedication. "I got a pint of strawberries over there for three fucking bucks kid," the bartender says. The meat guy has a voice like an ice pick, and like the rest of the regulars in here he's drinking with his own beer cozy around his bottle.

Here's a good one, he tells me. "What's the difference between a blonde and a washing machine?" Um. I don't know, I say. Something tells me this story isn't exactly going to turn out in the blonde's favor though. Just a hunch. "A washing machine doesn't follow you home after you drop a load in it." The bartender is not a blonde, I should point out.

She's going out for a smoke after the laughter dies down. Everyone else follows her out. Before she leaves she checks in on me one more time. "I hate to leave people hanging she says." All of a sudden I'm utterly alone in an unfamiliar bar in an unfamiliar part of the city. It's kind of nice. I've got a cold beer, a baseball game on, and a bag of cheap Cheetos. What more is there? It's sort of peaceful like this. I feel like I own the place.

JAMAICA PLAIN/ROSLINDALE

BK's

4272 Washington St., Roslindale
Phone: 617-323-9191

Dive Bar Rating

I was just doing a search for BK's online and the first thing that came up was this headline: "Cocaine being sold out of BK's Pub in Roslindale." So naturally, as an investigative reporter, I wanted to go, uh, check out the scene. Turns out there have been a few coke busts over the past couple years. I'm not a criminal mastermind, but I'd say it's a pretty good bet that after the second or third undercover sting operation at the bar, it might be a good idea to put that shit on hold for a minute. Just saying.

None of that would be even remotely surprising once you step foot in this railroad apartment style bar on the outskirts of Rozzie Sq. "Home of the Brave" reads the sign over the door. You've got that right, sign. I had to man up just to cross the threshold. BK's practically has a glowing neon sign that says "ex-cons welcome", flashing in the window.

Note to filmmakers looking to do a period piece in Boston, this part of Roslindale looks like it's straight out of the sixties. There's a divey laundromat, an ancient public library annex and an array of other businesses that seemed airdropped in from the past. This is the part of the city where Boston starts to get a little weird. There are lots of trees and birds chirping, and families walking around doing family stuff, but it's somehow more urban than downtown.

The bar room looks like your dad's shitty first apartment. There's a little kitchenette up front, which I hope no one uses, and, strangely, a plate of cheese and crackers laid out for people to pick at. It reeks of cigarettes in here, and everything feels, smells, and looks green. One of the bartenders is pregnant, the other is an old fella who likes to crack-wise with the "young" ladies at the bar. There are very few sleeves on the shirts people are wearing in this bar, which is sort of notable.

Above the bar there are rows of washed-out polaroids of children next to the rolls of scratchies. I don't think they were taken with the my hipstamatic for iPhone, but then again I didn't get a close look. What are people talking about in here? Like you even need to ask.

The Red Sox and Dunkin Donuts. Everyone loves to complain about both. One guy couldn't get his order made correctly no matter what he did. I know the feeling. "This was an American, by the way," he says, putting everyone at ease. "Everyone thinks it's a foreigner. It took me five times to get my order right." One of the ladies says her friend gets one with ten sugars. "Oh, that's a heroin addict right there."

Everyone is so happy in here though. It's the difference between a bar where neighborhood guys go to get drunk at, and a bar that is the only place that anyone in the neighborhood has ever, or will ever go to get drunk at, male or female. That mingling of genders makes a difference. Nonetheless, I feel a general sense of menace in here. Like everything could turn to shit, and someone could burst through the front door with a machine gun just like that. I'm pretty surprised one of the Afflecks hasn't played a plucky, good-hearted character that drinks here and gets mixed up in something he can't control. That sounds like something someone who only knows Boston from the movies would say, but this place is so real it's beyond fake. In this case the truth is stranger than fiction.

Cottage Tavern

1227 Hyde Park Ave., Hyde Park
No phone

Dive Bar Rating

I'd really love to tell you more about this temple of dive simplicity, but there's a couple things that are throwing me off here. First of all, I only found it because I was on my way to the classic Hyde Park Pub across the street, which, woops, turns out to have gone under recently. Another one bites the dust, I guess. Also, I was, as they say, hammered, when I got over here, so the night is a bit of a blur. And lastly, this is like the 110th dive bar I've been to recently, not to mention another 75 or so I've had to check out for my day job of reviewing bars for the *Globe*, *Stuff* and the *Metro*, so, to be honest, I'm really running out of ways to distinguish between these places. Cut me some slack, dude. On top of that, I don't even really know what this place is called. The faux-lamp post sign out front says Cottage Cafe, but inside the signs call it Cottage Tavern. Complicating matters further, it's neither a cafe, nor a tavern. (Discuss amongst yourselves).

A couple things I can tell you though: there's a shocking amount of young people in here, and not of the ironic dive-going sort either. It's a rainy Thursday night, and the neighborhood kids—vaguely threatening, mostly Irish, all wasted—are lined up at the bar bullshitting and flirting and doing the same old shit that people everywhere do. It just seems slightly different here, because it's an unfamiliar neighborhood. I'm still not really clear what Hyde Park even is. Ok, sort of kidding. It's a remote southern neighborhood of Boston with a diverse demographic or black, hispanic and Italian and Irish immigrants. So, basically it's like every other outlying Boston neighborhood that are the best places to find the realest dives.

I know I said that it's not like a cottage, but I guess if you look at it through beer-goggles, it seems like it could be. It's all bright wood paneling with homey faux-wood etchings lining the walls: old-timey tennis matches and golfers and idyllic sporting scenes from a bygone, innocent era. It's a square, boxy room, with a pool table, juke box, Keno and a snack vending machine that looks like it hasn't been restocked in years. That won't stop me from dialing up some crackers. Fearless adventurer over here, living life on the edge. The cuteish blonde Irish bartender doesn't like me though, so that makes me feel a little better.

Speaking of the juke box, the girls down at the end of the bar are pumping money into it all night, blazing hip hop and pop r&b jams. If you had told me I was gonna be listening to Jay Z and Beyonce tracks all night when I was cautiously approaching this bar earlier instead of getting murdered in the face, I wouldn't have taken those odds. I'm not sure which would be worse. Can't you hear all of these songs literally every second of every day on every single radio station ever? After what seems like hours of that, the soundtrack makes an abrupt turn into pop-country. The girls start dancing, their boyfriends stand nearby punching each other in the arm and calling each other fag, or whatever it is normal guys do, and Toby Keith brings it all together with a song that sums up this place nicely. "We got winners, we got losers, chain smokers and boozers. We got yuppies, we got bikers, we got thirsty hitchhikers. And the girls next door dress up like movie stars. Mmmm, I love this bar."

The Drinking Fountain

3520 Washington St., Jamaica Plain
Phone: 617-522-3424

Dive Bar Rating

🍾🍾🍾🍾🍾

The Washington Street Elevated was torn down in 1987, but for some eighty years it was a central artery way for workers from Dudley Square and Forest Hills to travel into the city. The Forest Hills stop, just down Washington from the Fountain, has been rerouted into the Orange Line which now cuts through the city along the Southwest corridor and out into the northern suburbs. You can find evidence of the El's looming presence, winding its way into the city and over this notorious dive bar in framed photos on the walls from the seventies. You can also find a photo of Larry Bird mixing it up in an on the court brouhaha. Somewhere between those two historical moments you can discern the spiritual essence of the Drinking Fountain's lot in boozey purgatory.

Although it comes on a particularly fertile dive-hopping path that leads from Doyle's to JJ Foley's, and a dense residential community, it's situated on the edge of the relatively wooded, hilly Forest Hills, making it feel from some vantages like a lonesome, distant outpost for drinking trekkers. Step outside for a smoke, where you'll find plenty of company, and you can survey the athletic fields of Boston English High School, the school originally founded in 1821 as a place for working class children with trade-driven futures. The Fountain hues close to that blue collar outlook, which lends the space much of its vaguely threatening charm. Although charm might be a relative term if you find yourself on the business end of the type of good old fashioned beat down that seems likely to break out at any moment here. A group of track suited gold chain types jostling with a bilingual crowd look like they'd be equally as comfortable kicking a dude in the face as they would a soccer ball.

Aside from being a working class community, Jamaica Plain also happens to be a thriving arts and counter-culture center of the city, something like the Williamsburg or Echo Park of Boston, where young hipsters rub up against immigrant families and workers. It's proximity to Roxbury also makes it diverse racially. That means you'll find archetypes from nearly any group, ethnicity or class-wise tipping them back here. The racial balance was particularly surprising on the night I stopped in last. Sort of a cross between *Boondock Saints* and *The Wire*. Crumpled old Irish fellows with their crumpled old Keno tickets and blinged out black dudes shooting stick in the back. Down the long bar red-faced townies screamed at one another under a sign that laid out the tenants of Irish Diplomacy: "The ability to tell a man to go to hell so that he looks forward to the trip." That's pretty much how the shamrock turtleneck bartender treated me with his oppressive indifference. What did I expect, a round of applause for strolling in? It's still unclear how that maxim jibes with the sign on the wall next to it: "Be nice or go away."

Galway House

720 Centre St, Jamaica Plain
Phone: 617-524-9677

Dive Bar Rating

In *All Souls*, Boston author Michael Patrick McDonald's book about growing up poor and Irish in the 1970s, he captures what it was like living in a JP much different than the one you'll find today. When he was a child, his struggling mother would go bar to bar at night with her old accordion trying to make some extra money for groceries. One of the ones they came to was Galway House. "I'd listen to my mother from a barstool, along with all the old drinkers who were slouched over mouthing the lyrics between long cigarette drags," he writes. "I'd wait until one of them would notice me and offer to buy me some chips or a pickled egg from the big jar I was staring at."

Today there aren't any paupers, or pickled eggs around, but everything else seems like it hasn't changed in decades. You can't smoke inside anymore of course, but the patrons don't seem to have kicked the habit. The streets out front are littered with dozens and dozens of discarded butts. From out there the bar looks like a busted out shell. Jamie, a musician who has been coming here since about 1995 says that's part of the allure. "The place looks terrible from the front with the sometimes broken green Galway House sign and non descript brown door. But inside it is the typical old Boston bar layout."

"You can meet a whole range of people in here," he says. " Many come in to watch the Sox or the Pats. One guy to your left could be impeccably dressed and obviously well off, while on the other side would be a crazy bag lady. You'd meet people just in from Ireland, plumbers, electricians, students, and old retirees with great stories of old Jamaica Plan. You can go in for lunch for a quick bite and a beer at noon on a Thursday and see the same guys in there at 5 or 6 that afternoon."

JP is still yet to be completely gentrified, but the Galway represents its lingering grittier half, even if it's not a dangerous place by any stretch. It's a family style grit, just like in McDonald's day.

Zack, another musician who's spent a lot of time here has a slightly less rosy take. "The place is ok, not really a 'dive' dive," he says. "You're not gonna get killed or anything."

"It kind of has a pee sanitizer smell," he continues. "The bathroom has certainly seen a coke deal or three. What makes this a dive is townies, bad rec room lighting, smelly old carpets, cheap bottles, friendly old man bartender, and an occasionally higher than normal dirtbags quotient for the area."

The long room here is split in half by a tall divider, with a dining room on one side, and the bar on the other. Elderly couples, black and white, eat fried dinners on one half, while wrinkled veterans and rocker types drink on the other. True to its name, the bar is festooned with all sorts of gimmicky shamrocks, and green Christmas lights dangle from the ceiling. White plank board walls with green stripes are decked out with black and white photos of Marilyn Monroe, The Three Stooges and Jim Morrison, all of whom probably had a few good dive bars stories in them. There are so many bullshit little statues and knickknacks and the like behind the bar it looks like a midway Carnival game set up. This is about as good a representation of what JP used to be like as you're going to find. Everyone from the old neighborhood who's still alive, or around, is still coming in, but the new blood is too. All souls welcome, you might say.

JJ Foley's Fireside Tavern

30 Hyde Park Ave., Jamaica Plain
No phone

In the Mt. Rushmore of Boston dive bars, this outpost of the historic Foley's collection of bars is probably Teddy Roosevelt. Mostly because old Teddy spoke softly and carried a big stick. And he had a bad ass mustache. It's across from the leafy Forest Hills area, on a piece of road that is probably your best bet for dive bar crawling in the area, but don't be surprised if you get spooked walking in here late at night. The street was quiet, and the woods seemed ominous on a recent Sunday when I came in. I headed straight for the bathroom (on account of that aforementioned dive crawl) and talked myself into thinking this place was a lot scarier than it was. The industrial-sized basin sink in the men's room looked like it should have had a chopped-up co-ed torso marinating in it. Out in the front, it's a lot more welcoming though, even if it doesn't seem like it at first.

The big open space is taken up by a five sided island bar with rotating diner style bar stools. There is a fireplace, but it's not in use. Over the hearth there are huge trophies and an Irish and American flag, but as far as dive bars go, this one is sparsely decorated, minimalist almost. It's unsettling in a way. It looks rather like a Knights of Columbus hall in here, the type of place you'd go to celebrate your grandfather's 85th birthday.

You'll usually find a motley collection of old bearded locals and an ever-fluctuating lineup of twenty somethings grooving on the run down feel of the joint at night. Since it's such a legendary "dive bar", particularly for this JP area, the kids have adopted it to a certain extent, but it's still the real deal. There's a pin ball machine and dartboards, but they aren't "pin ball machines" and "dartboards." Baby mamas, would-be gangsters and the lesbian scene like it here too. "It's the strangest place," says Mike, a bartender from one of my favorite spots in Newton (a repurposed dive) called The Biltmore. He lives around the way. "It's a super divey, old towny bar, but the JP queer scene all hangs out there."

Dave, the bartender here, might not be mixing his own bitters and pickling onions or whatever the hip bartenders are doing now at bars like The Biltmore, but he's one of the city's classics. He's friendly, and professional, and loves to talk about sports trivia. Like the bartenders at all the Foley's locations he's always dressed in a white shirt, black pants and tie. I order a Miller Light bottle, and he sets me up with one of those six ounce glasses to pour it in you see at old dive bars and absolutely nowhere else anymore. After seeing guys drink their beers this way at like twenty different dives, I figure there must be a reason for it.

"Up until fifteen years ago, this is the only glass you'd need in your neighborhood bars. Now, the old timers come in, they pour their bottle of beer into that and they get exactly two full glasses. Then you'd do your mixed drinks in those as well. You'd fill it up three quarters with ice, then pour the booze until it covered the ice. Then you'd add your juice or your mixer to the top." The reason for that, he says, is that it just makes a better drink in terms of proportion of booze to mixer. "Bars use bigger glasses now, so it's all off." Since that was the only glass in stock, before the pilsner glass became popular, the old timers just got into the habit of using them. Now they don't want to change. Things taste better the way you know them the best.

Midway Cafe

3496 Washington St., Jamaica Plain
Phone: . 617-524-9038

Dive Bar Rating

Like the best rock and roll dives, the Midway is tiny, gritty, and covered from stem to stern in stickers and photos of the thousands of bands who've been spitting out their punchy dive rock here over the years. The room is thin and the stage is small. So are the bands, which for anyone with a working heart and ears are the best kind. Ok, maybe not always on the ears.

The Midway is the trashy torn knee in the skinny jeans of the city. It's also consistently voted one of the best gay and lesbian hang-out spots in the city papers. The only thing queer in sight last time I stopped in was the cocktail of choice of a couple of sorority girls ordering a sex on the beach at the bar. "It's ok, you don't have to make it," their boyfriend said to the surly bar man. He didn't know what was in it anyway. Somehow he ended up pouring a shot of Jim Beam by mistake, which he sent my way. Forget what I said about him being surly.

It's freezing in here while I'm waiting for the crowd for that night's show to roll in. Rock clubs rely on body warmth to heat the place in the winter. It's also thick with that tangy air of disinfectant and potential that fills a rock club in anticipation of go time.

I try to strike up a conversation with the bartender. He doesn't want to give me his real name. His contempt for my questions is awesome to behold. I spend a lot of time writing about higher end bars and restaurants for the *Globe*. The type of places with publicists who bend over backwards to try to get me to mention their clients and managers who are desperate for press. One sign of a dive is how little they give a shit about the presence of a potential reviewer.

David Balerna, who has owned the bar with his brother Jay since 1987 is more forthcoming. Through some sort of Jedi power of suggestion type move the bartender got me on the phone with him while I was sitting at the bar. "I was the youngest bar owner in the city of Boston when we opened," Balerna says. "But that's passed me by now."

So what's changed over the years since then? "Just what we book.

We went from blues to rockabilly, to ska, to the screamy, nasty stuff for a while." Now it's a mix of punk, indie rock and gay and lesbian theme nights.

"It came to a point that was so evident that there was a need for it," he says of the latter. "It was all about safety. You could throw a gay and lesbian night, but if it didn't feel safe it would fall on its face," he says.

Although Jamaica Plain has a large GLB and young rocker population, one drawback that remains is bringing people in from elsewhere in the city. The nearby Orange Line, like the rest of the MBTA system, stops running ridiculously early at night. "We're kind of between a rock and a hard place. We don't have the privilege of Cambridge, where people can go to TT's and see a band then go some place else." He's right. For people who don't live in JP it can often seem like you have to take a helicopter to get there. "I was thinking about running a shuttle back and forth to Allston at night."

"We still have a large crowd though," he says. "We've weathered the storm. We're the little rock club that could. Twenty two years later and we're still doing what we're doing."

Robyn's Bar and Grill

4195 Washington St., Roslindale
Phone: 617-323-6507

Dive Bar Rating

Not to get all Jeff Foxworthy on you here, but when the floor mats behind the bar have got as many bald spots worn into them as the heads sitting around the bar on a Monday afternoon, that's a pretty good sign you're at a dive bar. When you wander into a drunken sin-galong to Billy Joel's "It's Still Rock and Roll to Me" led by a four foot drunk with a sunburned head and a tank top on, that's a pretty good sign you're at a dive bar.

Another good sign is when you find yourself at a big bar like this that absolutely no one you know has ever heard of. Like everyone else who doesn't live over here, I got hopelessly lost driving around Roslindale. That's got to be one of my favorite parts about drinking out in neighborhoods I don't often get to for this book: finding an undiscovered gem. A diamond in the rough if you will. Or a turd in the rough is probably more accurate.

Inside it's a cavernous echoing room with some of the implied class that newish Irish taverns are hoping to borrow with their dark stained walls and exposed brick and distressed wood. But it seems like the shine came off real fast here. It looks like it's condemned from the outside, and it feels like it's a place for the condemned on the inside. That's a recipe for an awesome dive bar right there. It's only been open as Robyn's since 2007. Before that it was a place called the Game Day Pub, and before that Happy Hour.

When they took over, the new owners wanted to turn it into a family restaurant with a neighborhood bar attached. There are separate entrances for the two sides. The dining room connected to the bar is a carpeted function room that looks like a cross between a bingo hall and the continental breakfast room of the worst hotel you've ever stayed in, complete with old school coffee pot burner. Families do come here for dinner, but I wouldn't want to take my kids here, and they don't even exist. Maybe they'd like one of the weekly beer pong contests better, come to think of it. I'll have to remember this place when I have kids in like ten thousand years, although I have a feeling Robyn's might not even last until the time this book comes out.

Figurative kids seem to like it here though. They come in on the weekends for live music (not the cream of the crop musical talent it probably goes without saying), trivia nights and karaoke and all the other things that dive bars bait the booze trap with. The entertainment while I'm here isn't even up to that standard. The drunken singalong has moved on to "Crazy Train" by now. No one else but me seems to think this it's weird to be drinking next to wasted grown men singing at the top of their lungs in awful voices in the middle of the day. But like I said, I always get lost every time I come over to this part of the city.

Best Food

Rosebud Bar and Grill

On the Hill Tavern

El Mondonguito

Sonny's Adams Village Restaurant and Lounge

The Eire Pub

Portugalia

Pugliese Bar & Grill

Riverside Pizza

Newtowne Grille

Charlie's Kitchen

Delux Cafe

ROXBURY

Aga's Highland Tap

2128 Washington St, Roxbury
Phone: 617-427-6514

Depending on who you talk to, Aga's is either a unique gem in the heart of Roxbury, or else one of the worst bars you'll ever go to. It's all about perspective, you see. Suffice to say, everyone I asked wanted to talk about it—it's the type of place you don't soon forget. Possibly because everyone is shocked silly that a place like this even exists. My friend Zack cautioned me before I was heading over. "That is a horrible, horrible place," he said. "It's fully of saggy tits and c-sections." And that's something coming form him, because he's a total scumbag.

Boston is known for a lot of things, but strip clubs are not exactly high on the list. There are two downtown, and a few in the surrounding areas, but other than that Aga's is it. Through some loophole in the convoluted blue laws we've got here they've been allowed to stay open as a club that features "entertainment" of one sort or another. Whether that's all nude, topless, or the present day restrictions on "bikini only" depends on the shifting mood of the neighborhood people trying to get the place shut down for indecency or whatever else it is mother's cry about when they have nothing better to do.

·Granted, this area of Dudley Square has long been known as a pretty rough neighborhood, and clubs like this certainly do attract, how shall we say, a seedy, perverted element. But that doesn't have much to do with the girls at work. When was the last time you saw a guy with a boner try to stab anyone? With a knife, I mean, not his boner.

Inside it's dark, even by strip club standards. It smells like a beery rug when I come in, and faintly of ass. Like a strip club in other words. Strip clubs generally aren't my thing by the way. The constant sales pitch from the girls always depresses me. Who are you, Willy fucking Loman with implants over here? It's just gross. This place isn't really like that. I mean, it is gross, but you're not getting hit in the face with the hard sell, or with tits for that matter.

"This place is legendary," my colleague and fellow dive

aficionado Jeannie tells me. "It used to be a Greek family-owned jazz club dating back to the 40s. When the neighborhood started 'changing,' they started bringing in 'live entertainment.' Technically, it's not a strip club because the girls are supposed to have their nipples covered, but I'll be damned if it ain't the nastiest joint in town. The best part is that the mom is still the bartender, while the sons work alongside her and do the door."

Our friend Mick puts it another way. "If you really want a head trip go visit Aga's Highland Tap, the last remaining topless bar in the city. I went with Jeannie, a full on lesbian, in the middle of a crowd of almost entirely black folks, with the doorman and the ancient bartender, a woman, being the only other white folks in the place. No problem whatsoever. We settled in and watched, in order, an Asian, a black girl, a white girl and a Puerto Rican who must have weighed 200lbs dance at the stripper pole in the middle of the room. All the rest looked bored but the Puerto Rican was having fun." That's almost touching in its expression of diversity, and just goes to show the power that boobs, even bad ones, have in bringing us all together.

El Mondonguito

221 Dudley St., Roxbury
Phone: 617-522-3672

The name of this basement level bar room slash Puerto Rican takeout joint means "little tripe" in Spanish, but I'm pretty sure an alternate translation is "Oh great, here comes another gringo cultural tourist writing about how wacky our neighborhood spot is."

An awkwardly laid out little hole in the wall in what you might charitably describe as a sketchy neighborhood if you were sort of racist, but also, you know, telling the truth, it's pretty safe to say there aren't many places like this in the city. On the bottom floor of a standalone residential building ravaged by grafiti, and located next to a trash-strewn vacant lot, this is a locals favorite that caters to the PR community, young and old alike, as well as the occasional nervous bar writer.

It doesn't really seem like a bar in here, more like a take out spot with a few fold out tables and a long counter on one wall for balancing your Heineken. One wall is painted with a mural of a singing frog while the others feature rural paintings of Puerto Rican fields and the framed results of years of domino tournaments. You'll probably need to show up pretty frequently to be invited into one of those. In the front there's an old style CD jukebox loaded with merengue, bachata and so on, and a giant fan mixing the hot air from outside with the overwhelming smell of perfume.

There's no bar as such, but rather a counter window where they sling out bottled beers and take out food from a display window. It's mostly fried chicken and meat patties, rice and beans and other delicious PR staples (including, of course, tripe). There's no menu, but the girl behind the counter walked me through all the options when I asked. I thought I might stick out like a sore thumb here, and I certainly did, but no one seemed to give a shit. They've got the same stuff everywhere else in the world that we've got here in Boston: beer, meat, music and friends. The only difference is, when a festive salsa track comes on, you might see some of the clientele move to the middle of the floor to venture a few steps. It's not unheard of to find drinkers dancing in the middle of a dive in Boston, but how often is the dancing actually any good?

Pat "Packy" Connors Tavern

Dive Bar Rating

203-5 Blue Hill Ave., Roxbury
No phone

I believe the correct euphemism for Packy Connors is a "troubled" pub. There have been so many incidents of violence here over the years that Boston Police and the licensing board seem like they're always trying to shut it down. So how bad is it? A shooting here, a stabbing there? Not quite. The police have been called here over 100 times in the past five years. It's been closed down temporarily and reopened so many times you should probably check the crime blotter in the newspaper before coming over here just to make sure you're going to be able to get in. As it is, they've been forced to curtail their hours; closing time is now at midnight. So, problem solved, right?

The bar, which was opened back in the thirties, has the look, both inside and out, of an Irish tavern. That's mostly what it was throughout its long history. But after many of the other white owned businesses moved out of the area in the 1960s, it was gradually adopted by the African American community that moved into the neighborhood. It's now usually referred to as the "black Cheers" of Boston. Although I don't remember the part in Cheers where Norm got shot outside the bar.

Like the Dublin House just around the way, it's a curious mix of styles at Packy's, with both old entrenched Irish and African American cultures rubbing up against one another. That means ancient framed Bruins jerseys next to photos of Martin Luther King and local politician campaign signs on the walls of this huge space.

The bbq and soul food here are standouts though. It actually has the feel of a summer camp mess hall in a way. A really, really unfortunate summer camp. There are brown formica booths and ravaged tile floors, a long bar that leads to a deli counter in the back, hanging fake flowers, picnic tables, brown drop tile ceilings. There are no windows, and everything is painted dark, so it's very dim inside.

It's possible that I had no idea what a dive bar really was until I stepped foot in here. There's a birthday party of sorts going on here when I do, with a cake displayed on a big table in the middle of the room. It's a gathering spot for families by day, but plenty of the less desirable nighttime crowd mixes in as well. One crack zombie almost falls over onto my table as she stumbles through the room. In a *Boston Globe* story in 2009 after a high profile shooting outside the bar here, former Licensing Board Chairman Daniel F. Pokaski talks about how "he has seen other beloved neighborhood bars, places where 'everybody knows your name,' that became 'hellholes' after midnight." If that's not the perfect description of a true dive bar, then I don't know what else to say.

Some things you probably shouldn't say at a hard Boston dive bar

Is this bag of 25 cent Doritos locally grown and organic?

Dropkick Murphys suck.

What are you looking at, buddy?

Labor unions are an affront to democracy.

75% of the things I wrote in this book.

This place smells like my grandfather's balls.

Can you add some more cranberry juice to this Cosmo?

How come you don't have any Crystal Castles on the jukebox?

Bill Belichick is a cheater.

Anything.

SOMERVILLE

Casey's

171 Broadway, Somerville
Phone: 617-625-5195

Dive Bar Rating

The Winter Hill section of Somerville is iconic in Boston area history. Long stereotyped as a devout Catholic area where bathtub Virgin Mary statues on the front lawn are a common find, it's also become synonymous in underworld lore as the home base of Whitey Bulger and the Winter Hill Gang, the most notorious Irish mafia outfit in the city's history. Like anywhere else it's moved a long way from its roots in recent years, but by and large it's still a neighborhood untouched by over-development. Unreliable public transport, and a dearth of gentrified commercial areas make it a kind of neighborhood frozen in time like a bug trapped in amber. It's also one of the most densely populated and ethnically diverse areas around, and you can find evidence of this along Broadway, a major thoroughfare that cuts through Somerville on the way to Boston that was hugely important in the commercial development of both cities.

Whether or not anything underhanded went on in here in the past isn't talked about, but it's safe to say that there's comparatively little air of menace at Casey's today. Still, the reputation of the area persists. "You almost feel like you might catch a glimpse of Whitey Bulger on the right day," Lincoln, a musician who lives in the area told me. A locals-heavy dive with a dumpy exterior, it's bright and clean on the inside, and a lot friendlier than you'd expect. That welcoming demeanor is a testament to why some of Winter Hill's younger contingent has adopted Casey's as a safe dive to drink in.

I'm tucked into a corner table by the touchscreen video game drinking a cheap beer directly in the middle of the large room's two areas. On one side middle aged dudes in Sox jerseys are draining bottles in front of the game, on the other a table full of twenty something girls are laughing over a few gin and tonics. "There's a lot of old world Somerville in Casey's," says Lincoln. "I also like that Casey's is far enough into Winter Hill that the college kids are afraid to go."

No one's eating, so the tiny Asian cook is wandering around the room shaking hands with familiar faces. Everyone is talking about St.

Patrick's Day coming up next week. The walls are covered in flyers promoting the authentic Irish experience at Casey's, just like every other bar within two hundred miles. March in Boston bars is a lot like the frenzy of department stores in the run up to Christmas.

Over the course of a few beers it gets a little busier. People wander over to the jukebox and scratch ticket machine from time to time, but mostly we all sit here staring into our beers. It's miserable outside, a veritable hurricane, but everyone's made the trek out to the neighborhood watering hole anyway.

The group of old boys over at the next table all have those grim, Massachusetts faces that make me feel like I'm among family. This seems like the species of bar my grandmother might have dragged me to after a funeral or parade or some nonsense when I was really young. Maybe that's why I always feel like someone's going to get yelled at in a place like this: childhood flashbacks. A slow moving white hair wanders over to me and pretends to play the video game screen for a minute. He probably just wants to know what the asshole with the notebook is writing down. After a moment he turns back and walks off without saying anything. Lucky for me, I guess. Considering what happened to a lot of dudes who wrote down things they probably shouldn't have around here back in the day the stern look I got was a cakewalk.

Fasika

145-147 Broadway, Somerville
Phone: 617-628-9300

Dive Bar Rating

One of the best parts about researching for this book is when I stumble upon a dive that I had no idea was even there. Often times that makes for the most deliriously incongruent experiences, like at Fasika, the Ethiopian restaurant and dive bar just outside of Winter Hill on Broadway.

When you're looking for a dive bar, sometimes the best examples are right under your nose in ethnic restaurants you might only know of as take out spots if you've ever considered them at all. People do talk about the food here, although the space is such a hole in the wall that you'd probably have to work up a bit of courage to commit to the experience.

The room is painted in bright yellow, and the retractable screen doors between the bar side and the restaurant put me in mind of an authentic African cafe. Not that I've ever been to one mind you, but this is pretty much how I'd imagine it. Gently swaying ceiling fans, colorful decorative flourishes and tribal art on the walls. The brilliant conflation of culture here finds all of that sharing space with the predicable touches of dive bar Americana: Budweiser signs, Keno screens, scratch tickets, basketball on the TV. It's hard to tell if this is an African place touched by the insidious marketing arm of American capitalistic hegemony, or a sloppy American dive making a half-hearted effort toward its heritage. To paraphrase Tolstoy, all happy bars alike, but every unhappy bar is unhappy in its own way. Anyway, it's pretty safe to say you won't find other bars like this around here. Even if some of the dive touchstones seem familiar, they're colored with an exotic difference. A smattering of decorations throughout the restaurant side notwithstanding, this is a bare-bones operation. Almost suspiciously so. An Americanized version of this same bar would cover itself in décor like a pig rolling in shit. Fasika is austere, grim almost.

The African transplants drinking at the bar are happy though. Why not? It's quiet and peaceful. That is until a wasted, middle aged Somerville townie rolls in. She's loud, breaking up the entire vibe of the room, but apparently she's a regular presence. The Irish bartender (Irish? Come on, you couldn't find an African dude?) starts giving her shit. Then a hug. She's just in from the check cashing place nearby, and the hospital earlier that day. No offense to insane bitches, but this bitch is insane. She launches into a story about so and so being in the hospital and it occurs to me that a lot of the conversation I overhear in dive bars revolves around who is sick and who is dying. You don't hear that sort of thing in your fancier bars. Without making too convoluted a point about class here, it's a reminder of our fleshly impermanence that better-heeled drinkers aren't comfortable talking about in public. Death and sickness are obviously realities for everyone, but in a dive they're a more vocal, visceral reality. Maybe because the customer's tend to be old, maybe because they're too down to earth to feel like they need to keep it bottled up? Maybe rather because they're drunker and their inhibitions are down? People drink differently, people get sick differently, people talk about both differently. This place is just different. But it's also exactly the same.

On the Hill Tavern

499 Broadway, Somerville
Phone: 617-629-5302

Dive Bar Rating

🍾🍾🍾

On the Hill Tavern is located on the Somerville and Medford line at a six way intersection I've never passed through without having to give way to one form of siren-blazing car or another. There's a CVS on one side, a Dunkin Donuts on the other. Over there is a check cashing store. That's like the trifecta of scumbag loitering in Boston.

Not many scumbags on the inside, but plenty of local characters, you might call them. My friend Matt lives around the corner. He comes in for cheap Bud Light pitchers and what he says is decent food. "There is always this old dude who stands outside with a plastic police badge," he told me. "We call him the sheriff. He just stands on the corner by the door and smokes cigarettes. If you don't live in the area you'd probably think he was a bouncer."

"Another dude who goes there every Friday and Saturday wears a different team's hockey jersey and roots against every Boston sports team." OK, so maybe there are a few scumbags. That Boston hater brings up a good conundrum though, one that I've come to time and again over the course of my year long descent into debauchery: is this just a sports pub or is it a dive bar turned sports pub? With the sports bar arms race going on in Boston bars, forcing even the lowliest of watering holes to accumulate the sort of viewing arsenals formerly reserved for Pentagon war rooms and evil scientists' underground lairs it's hard to figure out where a lot of bars stand. So when you've got 25 flat screens contrasted with a scratch ticket machine and the type of bathroom you might expect someone to wake up in in one of the Saw films chained to the toilet, and the bartenders are picking out their Keno numbahs at the bar, things get a little confusing. Is it a shit hole here? Well, yeah, but it's a nice shit hole.

The funny thing about young people though is that they don't mind a shit hole. They prefer it a lot of times, if my apartments in my early twenties are any indication.

The space itself is cavernous with high ceilings and exposed ducts. I'd say more about the decor but it's kind of hard to concentrate on the details with the onslaught of TVs, video games and beer signs here. Good thing I'm not seizure prone. Not yet anyway, give me a few more cheap drafts and we'll talk.

The live entertainment is riveting as well. There's a pride of dudes huddled at one end of the room plotting whatever sort of ridiculousness guys with goatees and XL hoodies get up to nowadays. Although the crowd at the bar on my side of the large room wasn't entirely devoid of grey hairs. In fact the fella I sat next to drinking our $2.25 Bud Light drafts was sporting what is probably the only known example in nature of the ghostly white mullet.

The bartenders all looked like they might have been rejects from a reality show casting call. Just hot enough to do jello shots with, but ballsy enough to kick you in the nuts for getting smart. The over all feel here is the setting for the denouement of some vapid post-douche reality drama on VH1 actually. (Is there some quota for Boston a-holes on those things by the way? That shit is starting to give me a complex.)Meanwhile, the room is filling up and I'm warming to the crowd. This may be a menagerie of Boston douches, but these are my people. I'm a Boston douche myself after all.

(Tami Lee)

The Pub

682 Broadway, Somerville
Phone: 617-776-7373

Dive Bar Rating

Since the advent of the smoking ban in Boston a few years ago, it's not uncommon to have to fight your way through a gauntlet of smokers on the way into any bar. But the grim countenances of the type of smokers you'll find outside a place like this are more akin to gargoyles you'd see perched on a gothic cathedral. Inside things are a bit less spooky. That's in large part due to a remodeling overhaul the place underwent a couple years back. It used to be known as the Powder House Pub, and it was an infamous hangout for underage Tufts kids and the townies who tolerated them. Now it's simply a hangout for of-age Tufts kids and the townies who tolerate them.

The remodeling brought sharp, exposed brick walls, and cleaned up the space considerably. Knocking down the walls of an adjacent building greatly expanded the bar's perimeter. The generally spiffied-up sheen contrasts with the drop tile ceilings however, the intersection of which is a nice visible metaphor for the type of fence straddling a place like this does: one part town, one part gown. A lot more of the former were doing time at the bar on a Saturday night. Groups of blue collar joes and slumpy drinkers in dad jeans were yelling at the Notre Dame game on the TV. Devout Catholics, apparently. Later that night the kids would get shitty. Later that week maybe stop back in for trivia or karaoke.

If you were rolling past on a chilly Fall night you'd have no idea that they'd made renovations. Its Ball Square location– minor leagues as far as squares go—places it between Kelly's Diner and Soundbites, where you'll find lines of yuppies and sweatpants-wearing co-eds beaming over the prospect of their morning eggs. All dives should come attached at the hip to old school diners.

"This used to be the Ball Square Grill," the man seated next to me explained. He was complaining audibly about the price of his $3.25 Bud bottle. "It was a hole in the wall. This is going back twenty years now."

Seems like it's decked out for the college kids now, I said.

"The whole square is. That's Tufts. You're in yuppie town right now."

His name is Phil. He's a machinist and he's lived in this neighborhood his entire life. Dekkos was the place to go twenty years ago, he said. Then it was called Mulligan's. Both gone. The Genoa too. "Some of them ran into drug problems or whatever. They closed 'em down. Cocaine got 'em all." So why's he still here? It can't be for the Miley Cyrus jam playing over the speakers. Tradition, I suppose. Nowhere else to drink more likely.

"Somerville used to have a bar on every corner," he said. "Then the rich people moved in. What do they call that, progress?"

I met a late twenties neighborhood girl outside smoking a cigarette. "They made it look nice, but if you come here during the day it's the same people every day sitting in the same seats."

A gaggle of co-eds flitted through the doors. The Black Eyed Peas were on the stereo now. "Tonight's gonna be a good night." Yeah, it probably is for them. For me and Phil it was time to fade off into the night.

(Tami Lee)

P.A.'s Lounge

345 Somerville Ave., Somerville
Phone: 617-776-1557

Dive Bar Rating

Toward the thick nucleus of Somerville's bustling Union Square—which is somehow one of the most trafficked and hardest to access commercial and residential areas in the city—squats the boxy brick facade of P.A.'s Lounge. The name, Portuguese American's Lounge, makes sense in this largely Portuguese speaking, Brazilian enclave, although from the looks of the place you wouldn't be too off pronouncing it phonetically either—as in your pa's lounge. It seems like the type of place your dad might have hoisted a few jars with the boys after quitting time back when. These days you won't find too many fathers, or São Paulo transplants for that matter in here.

Sickly green lights throw a half-hearted shine against bright yellow walls riddled with a mix of license plates, framed magazine covers, sports memorabilia, comic books, beer mirrors and stylishly designed rock show flyers. That last bit explains the 100% dark rim bespectacled population last time I popped in. Beneath a layer of glass on the wooden bar decades-old sports cards imbue our $3 PBR sipping with an air of faded glory. Darryl Strawberry's forearms are looking good from this vantage. Meanwhile a cute redhead in Chuck Taylor's and leggings under her shorts is explaining the Fluff festival that just went down around the corner in Union. (The nasty stuff was invented right over here in 1917.) They had a Fluff cooking contest. Fluff beauty pageant (hair product apparently). Bands playing Fluff songs I guess. Anyway, that's Union Square, the crossroads of artsy bicycle enthusiasts and their quaint ironies. No surprise that they'd head to PA's ex post facto.

A band is loading onto the stage in the room adjacent to the bar. It's a hollow, elementary school gymnasium/ Knights of Columbus style venue that echoes like hell, but the kids swear it's the real deal. I'm casting sideways glances through the port hole windows on the bar side. Later tonight a modest crowd of local indie punks will assume their geometrical observation patterns in front of the small stage. Plenty of hot local talent throw down here on the way up and out and the occasional hot national punk act spits through. Peelander

Z, Japanther, Faces on Film, whoever.

Back at the bar the Fluff kids are laughing at Rick James looking smooth as ice in hip level red vinyl boots on a magazine cover framed on the wall. Herschel Walker and Jeremeny Roenick are staring back at me from the bar frozen in a moment of perpetual youth. The movement of young bodies around me, in front of me. A fat bearded comic book fan and his skinny buddy in a Member's Only jacket are cursing the Sox on the tube. Fucking Yankees again. A group of middle aged motorcycle cliches clomp in, all shoulders and leather. They're friendly and laughing with Gerry the manager, but they've at least introduced the idea of danger into the place. Now PA's has a little bit of everything.

Rosebud Bar and Grill

381 Summer St., Somerville
Phone: 617-440-6284

Dive Bar Rating

The Rosebud Diner is a long running Somerville institution, a classic tin train car diner that's been in business since 1941. The Bar and Grill on the other hand is relatively uncharted territory. It's cache seems to be on the rise, however, as spill-over drinkers from the other packed Davis Square bars have begun to take advantage of this big space. It's also become an anchor of the local bar rock scene in the past year.

"The bar has been there since the 1950s and it was actually a rock club in the 1980s called the Surrey Room," Jordan Valentine says. She was booking shows here for a while. "It was most recently an Italian restaurant but switched back to just a bar in April of 2009."

Paul Christie remembers the Surrey Room well, he tells me. He's been bartending in Davis Square at nearby Gargoyles (not a dive by any stretch) for about sixteen years. "The Surrey Room was black as night," Christie says. "All you could see was the illuminated shelves on one side and the dart board on the other."

A quick scan of the crowd on Saturday night when I stumbled through is a bit of a mixed bag. Grumpy looking grandmothers scowling at the world, old timers waiting for the clock to run out on the game (on TV and life), orange-tinted girls with Boston accents so thick you could get stuck in them, bald tough guys looking for an excuse to kick my ass and gambling addicts plying their video-driven trade. Did I just wander into a bar or one of my family reunions?

The bar is a handsome dark wood and the walls are hung with art deco and modernist prints. The ceilings are ornate, better suited for the kind of high society drawing room nervous ladies should be fainting in. Arching window framed mirrors further the already spacious room's implied size. Don't worry, none of that exactly classes up the joint. The absurd number of Keno tickets on the bar, bar-mounted video game and specials menus ($16 for a pitcher and an appetizer platter) see to that.

The dining room behind the bar is the real twist to this convoluted plot. It's a bright red carpet and vinyl booth nightclub/ diner / lounge hodgepodge that looks like it should be the setting for a broke ass wedding reception. Wraparound mirrors are spotted with glowing orbs that give off a rumpus room disco effect. It was probably the up to the minute style in nineteen seventy whatever.

The Irish bartender's mom is sitting nearby at the bar unimpressed as I scan the room over a pint of PBR that taste like swine flu. The room smells like floor disinfectant and pizza. A couple beers in, the sad-eyed waitress hasn't looked over at me enough and the linebacker door man has looked over too many times. I'm starting to like it here a lot all the same. It's like a vortex of space and time where the normal boundaries don't exist. Or better yet like you've put the entire history of bar culture on shuffle and just let the results play out as they will. I've got no idea what's going to happen next here. In the meantime another awful beer. You know, just in case.

Sligo Pub

237 Elm St., Somerville
Phone: 617-623-9561

There are plenty of bars in Boston named after authors, Bukowski Tavern, Flan O'Brien's and The Brendan Behan for example. And with the proliferation of bar stool scribblers in this city—souls poisoned by poetry and whiskey alike—it's not surprising to find plenty of fictional characters named after bars as well. Write what you know, right?

With the ear for drinkers' patois that Boston-based author Steve Almond has shown in story collections like *My Life in Heavy Metal* it's no surprise that the man knows his way around a dive or two. I asked him about his dive of choice for processing the fuel of pint to pen.

"My favorite was the Sligo, just outside Davis Square," he told me. The Sligo, like nearly everything else in town takes its name from an area in Ireland. "All the young pretties wound up at the Burren," the warehouse-sized Irish bar around the corner, "but the Sligo was where the serious alcoholics hung their tongues. It smelled like dead animals and accepted only cash, both qualities I find admirable in a dive." He's dead on about the smell. McKinnon's Meat Market is next door.

"I wound up writing a whole bunch of short stories starring a drunk named Sligo," Almond told me. He's a memorable character, equal parts boozy bluster and post-intellectual hard ass. Sligo, "had the manner of a man who'd just pulled an all-nighter at Caesar's Palace and walked into the dawn dead broke," reads one description in the story "What Were the Sophists." "He was a vicious smoker; already his voice sounded like a hedge trimmer."

You might uncover more than a few suspects matching that description at the Sligo. I'm not sure if this will disappoint Almond to hear, however, but these days, alongside those rugged types on a packed weekend night the place is absolutely rotten, (or fresh would make more sense I suppose), with young ladies. Here, like many dives, you get to see the circle of life metaphor reenacted anew each day as night comes and the old give up their space for the young. Good to see a few haggard soldiers tough it out amidst the crowd of kids though, remaining utterly indifferent to the flirtatious playacting going on around them. Everything they're interested in is stacked in rows on the other side of the bar anyway.

It's a truly curious place, and an odd match for the neighborhood. Davis Square is one of the younger, hipper areas of Somerville. The type of neighborhood an alien who's never been to Earth but has recently been introduced to the concept of counter-culture lesbians and read a few months worth of the local arts weekly would dream up if asked to describe an American city.

But the Sligo persists. Dive bars are like wounds on the body of the city, and patrons are like white blood cells flooding to the spot to fix it. Big crowds of drinkers breathe a bar back into health, sometimes leading to the type of gentrified renovations that cover up any evidence that the wound existed in the first place. But cut off that blood supply and it hardens into a crooked scar. In other words an unpopular dive remains a dive. Run a popular one and the owners start getting ideas. A steady influx of renewable college age drinkers hasn't had that healing effect on the Sligo however. The scar, as it were, remains. Sometimes literally. In fact many of the surfaces inside the long, narrow, cramped room are marked by years of amateur woodworking. Trace your fingers along the markings and you could read the lines like some liquored-up brail narrative. This one is filled with characters.

SOUTH BOSTON

Ace's High

551 Dorchester Ave., South Boston
Phone: 617-269-7637

Dive Bar Rating

🍾🍾🍾🍾

Andrew Square is something of a crossroads in Boston. Literally speaking it's home to a prominent Red Line stop, but its location at the axis of South Boston and Dorchester and its relative proximity to the South End make it a way station for a diverse cross section of Boston culture. To the west, the expressway thrums with heavy traffic puttering off to the suburbs, to the east is the grassy expanse of Columbus Park, and just beyond that the old Boston harbor. By road, by train, by sea, there are plenty of ways to get out of here, but for decades people have stayed mostly put.

Ah, but not for long, you're thinking. Too true. Across the street from this woefully overlooked dive bar gem sits a tall, newly built column of—you guessed it—luxury condos. This real estate is too valuable, and too close to downtown to remain undeveloped for long. Although the expanse of industrial wasteland abutting the block that Aces High sits on is something of an eyesore. Further along in a vast parking lot construction cranes line up in rows like metal dinosaurs off the clock. And while it's not exactly downtown Kabul over here, the square and the adjacent areas still see their fair share of crime; a 24 hour Dunkin Donuts knocked over repeatedly, a recent bank robbery and knifing or two.

So what does any of that have to do with Aces High? Everything, actually. This is the type of bar where you can feel the push and pull of opposing forces working on it from either end. On the one hand it's a total dive's dive, with old timers drinking away the day, rows of motorcycles parked out front, and a decades-old hang dog vibe about the room. On the other, it's a fairly popular spot among the younger area crowd on weekends, (although not on the level of the ironically adopted dive just yet.) Fluorescent ink board signs advertise frozen drink specials ($4.50), so apparently women must come here. They're probably wearing leather jackets, but still. Inside it's clean, sociable, and amenable to all sorts of friendly gatherings; there are well kept pool tables in the back room, a cute little backyard patio, and a sort of warm by way of random décor. After a while a lot of these dives start blending into one another, but this one stands out, yet another variation on a theme. The front room still has the original old diner style set up, with booths and bucket seats, but there are odd touches, like plastic flowers in vases on every table. Boat wheel chandeliers hang from the ceilings and there are quaint paintings of flowers and wine bottle on the walls. Most dives are decorated like the apartment of a bummy twenty something college dude who thinks "Well, I got this, uh, thing, I might as well lean it up over there." This one looks like that same apartment after his grandmother visited and decided he needed some of her old shit to liven the place up.

I'm tucked into one of the booths while a group of bikers and their old ladies are rocking out to a truly inspired collection of awful nu metal on the jukebox. On the TV the results of the health care vote in Congress are playing out. A few of the grizzled drinkers and the man-giant of a bartender are watching intently. This place is nowhere as rundown as they come for Southie, but I wouldn't be surprised if most of the people in here haven't seen the inside of a doctor's office in years, myself included. People drinking all day on a week day afternoon don't tend to make the best choices regarding their health.

I walk out of the bar a few PBRs later still not sure that the majority of the country's dive bar drinkers are going to end up getting health coverage starting later that week, and I'm feeling a little pessimistic about the world. Down the road to the left Dot Ave. is a straight shot into the heart of the city. Across the street there's a pest control business and the empty courtyard of the vacant condos just put up. There's a swirling maelstrom of trash on the front lawn, a black plastic bag undulating in circles in the wind. It's just turning and turning and not going anywhere.

Oh, but up the street a fancy doggy day care store just opened. So at least there's that.

The Connection

560 Dorchester Ave., South Boston
Phone: 617-268-4119

Dive Bar Rating

🍾🍾🍾

I don't care how many layers of dark stain you throw down on your nice hard wood bar, or how handsome the deep red hues of the painted walls, if your PBR comes served in a plastic cup for $2 from a guy in nylon running shorts with a tubercular cough, then you're a dive bar. Sorry, I don't make the rules. OK, so I do make the rules here, but let's not split hairs.

This is a dive in a pub's clothing. Like a cartoon hobo at a funeral, or a junkie at a family court date, you can see the gritty edges. There also seems to be some sort of cultural disconnect going on in here. It's an Irish sports dive, but there's a distinct Italian American motif at work with the "Goodfellas" posters and Rat Pack memorabilia everywhere, (old Sinatra, young Sinatra, arrested Sinatra).

This place has the potential to get crowded for big game nights, but it's regularly quiet, despite its Andrew Square locale, and largely still a locals hang. The sign behind the bar attests to that with an old joke: "Bartender's Phone Rates: Not here $1; On the way home $2; Just left $3; Haven't seen all day $4; Who? $5." That's as retro a dive philosophy I've seen in a while. If by retro you mean sexist. You see, in the old fashioned drinking world that's carried over into contemporary dive culture, men hate their wives who are all controlling shrews apparently. And since there's only one bar they could be at (the closest one to their house obviously) that's where they're gonna call to see why he's not home with the baby formula or newspaper sleeve of bacon.

Dan is a bartender in the South End who lives around the corner. He's 30 and hip, and a relative late comer to this neighborhood. I ask him about how he fits in to the bigger picture of bars like the Connection.

"The neighborhood has definitely changed in recent years, there's many more condos and 'luxury' buildings as opposed to old triple deckers that an entire family lives in," he tells me. "Particularly my area has changed as it's a lot of industrial lots that are being converted."

And yet, he says, "the stereotypes aren't as harsh as they used to be when I moved to Boston in 2002, but they still cling. It's still considered a very blue collar town, with Irish everywhere and sections that you don't want to visit. There are definitely a good amount of places that are 'rough' and that I have no desire to visit." The Connection doesn't really qualify in that regard. But it's not the type of place you want to go running your mouth either. "People visiting a dive have to understand that although they think it's cool that they are 'slumming it,' this is someone's every day bar."

"Most of these little spots have the same group of regulars who don't want any outsiders. They are not trying to make a million, they just want to be left alone. Lots of old time Southie residents feel as if their neighborhood is suddenly being hijacked by developers and 'yuppies' who want an affordable condo."

(Kelsey Marie Bell)

The Corner Tavern

645 E 2nd St., South Boston
Phone: 617-269-9891

This dive on the bottom floor of an iconic Southie block of triple deckers is one of the most mismatched and haphazardly arranged bar rooms I've encountered yet. It's like a post-apocalyptic airport waiting lounge with its randomly collected industrial furniture, a bank of old style televisions in a row, most of which don't work, and a monstrously cracked floor. It's a few doors down from the Shannon, which I've just come from, and it makes that place look like a gleaming edifice of high end capitalism in comparison. Aside from the nice steel bar rimmed by a lightly stained wood ledge, you could mistake this for a guerilla operation set up in different living rooms on the fly every night.

"We are what we are," Mike the owner tells me from his perch at the bar. "We're known as a 'locals' place. It's a little dilapidated." That's an understatement, but there's a weary charm to his confession. He's proud of his bar. "No one has owned a bar in South Boston for as long as I have." Since 1980 he says.

I mention that a friend of mine lives in a beautiful loft nearby and that I'd love to move over here myself. Partly because it's true, but also because I've been talking about the effects of newcomers on the character of Southie so much lately I want to know what it's like to pose as the very change agent many of these bars are dealing with all the time. Sharon the bartender is all for it. She loves the area. Loves her bar too. "It's been here a long time," she says, emphasis on the long. She's got a pack a day voice and the type of accent that films about Boston so often try to capture but never can. "We never have any problems here, which is a priority. It's just local guys."

"It's so expensive over here to buy now though. But the great thing about Southie is that it's all right there in the neighborhood. You can walk to everything. The supermarket is right there, stores, bars. The only problem is parking. If you don't get a spot by six it's over."

She's playing good cop to Mike's bad cop. He's talking like a business owner happy for an influx of potential customers, but his demeanor tells me guys like me don't belong. Or maybe he's sincere. Hard to tell. "Twenty five years ago I wouldn't have known you," he says. "You probably weren't even born." Well, I was, but thanks for guessing me young.

How has he stayed in business so long, I ask? I'm drinking a Miller Light for $2.75. Takes a lot of those stacked end to end to fund a bar. "We offer a reasonable product at a reasonable price."

"And they're cold!" Sharon says. She's brought that up a couple times. Are there bars around where the beer isn't cold? Seems like a given, but I have to admit she's right, it is really cold.

"It is what it is," Mike says, back on the subject of Southie "Nobody cares," he says. "Nobody cares."

"I hope you move in. I hope it works out for you. Things change, life goes on," he says. "Ob-La-Di, Ob-La-Da."

(*Kelsey Marie Bell*)

Cornerstone Pub

16 West Broadway, South Boston
Phone: 617-268-7158

Dive Bar Rating

Our mothers used to tell us all sorts of made up stuff didn't they? Stuff like "You can do whatever you set your mind to if you try hard enough." and "That man is your father." You know, mother stuff.

Remember the thing she used to say about making weird faces all the time? "If you keep making that weird face it's gonna get stuck like that." Totally bullshit, of course, but pretty sound logic all the same. The essence of that theory is basically what's going on behind karaoke at dive bars. This sort of thing happens all the time. You start off doing something because it's funny or ironic. You're not bowling, you're "Bowling." Or maybe you're "Drinking Yourself To Sleep Every Night To Dull The Pain." It's funny that way, see?

A few years back I started adopting ironic Massachusetts townie slang, because, haha, people like that sound stupid. Woops. Now I say "What's up kehd" when my grandmother calls on the phone, and let it slip to my boss how fucking retahded I got at the bar last night.

Inertia and habit have a way of taking over and all of a sudden you've actually become something ridiculous you never intended to be, like a parent, or a person with a real job, or a sixty year old guy who's literally the only one in a Southie dive bar doing karaoke at 10 pm on a Thursday night. Karaoke is a lot like sex, and, I don't know, basketball. You can do it yourself, sure, but it's a lot better when there are other people involved. (Or so I'm told.)

So here's our man singing his heart out to "Across the Universe" by the Beatles. It's one of my favorites actually, and he's not doing too badly. But what the fuck? This is a bar located directly across from the Broadway T stop in drinker-heavy Southie on a Thursday night. It's deader than dog shit in here. Dead up and down the block everywhere I've been, sure, but nothing this bad. I've always thought of this place as a hot spot for young dive-hunting Southie kids. Not until midnight apparently, the bartender tells me. Not going out until midnight in Boston makes no sense by the way. That leaves very little time to get drunk and even less time to get in a fight.

Halfway through the song the karaoke host joins in on harmonies.

The three other people at the bar punching away at the touch screen video game turn up and look for a minute. I am melting into my seat in embarrassment. Not because I'm too good for this, mind you. I am exactly the right amount of good for this. It's just eye-opening. I am awe-struck by loneliness in fact. There's a sign above me in the corner by the scratch ticket machine that says "Beauty is only skin deep. Ugly goes to the bone." I feel ugly in here. Ugly in a good way. The host lifts my spirits a bit when she kicks into "Maybe I'm Amazed." She sings it pretty well. It's not pretty, but it's hitting all the right notes.

So, anyway, that's karaoke in a nutshell. Turns out mom was right when she said "If you keep making that weird face it's gonna get stuck like that." Except by face she meant life.

(Kelsey Marie Bell)

Croke Park/ Whitey's

268 West Broadway, South Boston
Phone: 617-464-4869

Dive Bar Rating

Sometimes called the Green Bar because of its bright green facade, and the fact that there is no signage out front, you probably wouldn't even realize that there was a place of business here if you didn't follow the tell-tale signs of early morning drinkers queued up on the sidewalk puffing butts with urgency, itching to get back to the cheap $1.50 pints of draft waiting for them inside. And what an inside it is: cold, hard brick for cold, hard drinkers. In fact if it weren't for the pool tables, popcorn machine, video games and TVs, you might think you were actually drinking outside in a sketchy alley between two decrepit brick walls. You could describe the folks inside as decrepit too, if you were the judgmental sort. In short, it's a shell of a bar, inhabited by the shells of neighborhood drinkers who treat this long standing spot like a second home. Some are comatose and near flat-lining at the bar, like the argyle sweater-wearing 40ish woman mumbling to herself and wobbling off her stool, and others are bursting with energy. Too much energy. Two hyper youngish dudes in retro track suit gear are shooting pool in violent, sudden bursts of movement that shock me with every stroke. It's not hard to imagine a scenario where one of those pool cues ends up against the back of my skull. Lest any of that scare you off, you'll occasionally still find plenty of enthusiastic post-college kids who are still really excited about the idea of drinking next to old people in bad jeans who swear by this place.

For years this spot was called Whitey's Place, but probably not the Whitey you're thinking of. Robert "Whitey" McGrail was a neighborhood bookie, although his reputation was far less fearsome than the area's most famous criminal Whitey Bulger. In 1985 he was shot to death inside the bar, allegedly over a gambling debt. No connection to Bulger was ever proved, but that's how things used to roll in Southie. Nobody said nothing. Not if they knew what was good for them. That's still good advice to take in any of these bars here. Or anywhere else for that matter.

Croke Park, by the way, one of the largest sporting stadiums in Ireland, was the site of the Bloody Sunday incident in 1920 when British troops opened fire on the crowd at a football match killing fourteen. Perhaps the name of the bar here alludes to that history in a defiant gesture. Perhaps they just like sports. You can probably figure that one out on your own.

There are no sports on when we come in, which is practically the raison detre for bars in Boston, so we're all content to stare blankly at the movie while the clank of pool balls and grunts of exertion play out behind us. Interestingly, only one of the three TVs is of the newer HD variety. The other two are boxy, old models with a fuzzy, off-color picture broken up by static. It occurs to me sitting here, sipping my beer, that this is what we all have to look forward to, both in terms of bars, and our own lives as well: being replaced by the newer model. Some of us will give way easily, others will cling to that which we know, unwilling to go without a fight. As Southie changes this seems like the type of place that isn't likely to go quietly. It's the old boxy TV of bars, showing the same thing as the HD set that popped up next to it, but creaking with its evident age. Eventually the picture will fade and everything will go to black, but not tonight.

Kiley's Tavern

138 Old Colony Ave., South Boston
No phone

Dive Bar Rating

🍾🍾🍾🍾🍾

"Where are you from," the bartender asks me. It's a loaded question in a lot of Boston bars, but particularly in what's leftover of the traditionally blue-collar enclave of South Boston. He's got a neck tattoo and looks like he knows how to use it. I pause for a minute trying to think about the right answer here. Actually, in a bar like this, there's really only one right answer: "From down the block." I consider bullshitting for a second, but realize I'm probably not gonna be able to pull that one off. "I'm from Watertown," I say. Watertown might as well be the other side of the moon. Not that he's trying to intimidate me, (although it's working all the same). He's polite, and quick with a bottle of Bud. His patrons on the other hand...

It's a couple days after St. Patrick's Day, and from the looks of this rugged crew at the bar I wouldn't be surprised if they'd been locked in here the entire time. The air is soupy thick with booze and aggression. I often joke about feeling out of place in some of these dives here, but this is one of the only times I'm actually a little bit worried about a fight breaking out. Not with me involved necessarily, but these things have a gravitational pull, like a cartoon tornado picking up everything in its path.

The gang seems content to keep their verbal sparring insular for now, although I don't know if you'd exactly call screaming "fuck you" across the room every thirty seconds insular. Everyone knows each other's names though, so it helps the curses land specifically. First name Fucking, last name something Catholic. Each of them seems on the verge of being thrown out too. Some already have been, but bar ejections, particularly with regulars who are used to it, take a little while to sink in. Leaving instantly once you've been cut off is like an easy defeat. Quietly defiant lingering is one's only reasonable recourse. Then again, too much resistance and a bartender like this is gonna put you on your ass. They're quietly strong, serious men in here, like John Wayne and Ted Williams who are looking down on us from framed posters on the walls.

I slink into one of the tables on the upper level of the room by the bathrooms and watch the March Madness tournament play out. Proper title for a sporting event here I'm thinking. They've got their own tournaments here as well, the bartender tells me when we both step out for a smoke onto the back patio. There's a horseshoe pit enclosed within a grim sort of industrial back yard fenced in on one side by the towering steel blue wall of an adjacent glass installation business. On the other side condos of course. "The regulars have tournaments back here in the summertime," he says. "People hear about it a lot on the internet now and they come down." They've got a Twitter account for Kiley's, which is the greatest, most unlikely thing I've heard all day. "@Southiedrunks Tommy's pissed at the bar" perhaps?

It's not the ideal backyard to throw shoes in, but it's kind of pleasant with a couple of picnic tables to sit on. Probably a nice spot to hang with the guys from the neighborhood. You make do with what you have. Someone is yelling from inside the door, so our conversation is cut short. "Who the fuck are you!?" the voice screams. "Get this fucking guy out of here." For a moment I'm sure they're talking about me.

Murphy's Law

837 Summer St., Boston
Phone: 617-269-6667

Dive Bar Rating

According to Murphy's Law, given enough time, pretty much anything that might go wrong in any given situation can and will. One thing the old adage doesn't mention however is that you can really speed that process along by the decisions that you make. For example, showing up to this Southie waterfront dive anytime around 1 am. Since it's one of the only bars in the area to stay open until 2 am, it's the place that all of the other bars nearby—and there are many —empty into before last call. Sloppy, late night Southie drinkers looking to force one or two more down the hatch before the end of the night all rolling in at the same time sounds like a sure fire recipe for shit going majorly wrong. You could say the same of pretty much any dive around last call though, so it's no reason to avoid this classic. We simply prefer to come by earlier in the evening when the crowd is made up of old timers drinking quietly at the bar and goofy twenty somethings snapping photos of themselves in the bar from *Gone Baby Gone*.

Yep, scenes from the Ben Affleck film were filmed here back in 2006. They're pretty excited about it here still, and will pull out the photo album for anyone who shows an interest. The excitement is understandable. In Boston pop culture terms Ben showing up to your bar to make a movie is only a close second behind Tom Brady and Aerosmith popping in for an impromptu jam session/game of catch.

Located on a ghostly quiet, wind-swept dead zone near the waterfront, Murphy's isn't exactly the type of place you'd like to find yourself lost at night. And make no mistake, if you don't know the streets over here, you will get lost. Quiet factories loom on nearby blocks, across the street in fenced in holding lots rows of stone kitchen tops stand like the scene of a well organized earthquake. Next to that is a lot full of giant steel girders likely waiting to be employed in the construction of one of the dozens of new lofts cropping up all over the neighborhood. So this is where gentrification is born!

Adjacent to the bar is a bus parking lot. Not sure if you've spent a lot of time loitering around bus parking lots, but they aren't usually located in the best part of town. Inside the bar it's a lot more homey in bright greens and reds. The walls behind the bar are decked out with crinkled, aging photos of patrons probably long since passed mixed in with younger children's school photos. The next generation of Murphy's drinkers in training perhaps? It's the circle of dive life on display.

The name of the bar can be taken in another, more literal sense as well. This place, like a lot of the other nearby bars, is basically a Dropkick Murphy's song come to life. The Dropkicks are the official poet laureates of Boston drinking culture; blue-collar, whiskey-throated Irish-Americans with bagpipes in their DNA and lager in their veins. Coincidentally, or predictably perhaps, the band comes up in conversation at the bar. A local couple is chatting up the bar man about music. Husband is Irish and indecipherable, paging impatiently through the Herald on the bar (dive bars read the Herald, by the way, not the Globe). She's strident and loud and direct, like the best stereotypical Boston women. Her granddaughter goes to school with the Dropkicks' singer's daughter, she boasts, which if you went into a science lab to pinpoint the exact type of thing you'd expect a grandmother in South Boston to brag about, besides their grandson going to BC, it's pretty much spot on. The talk turns to other Irish bands. The Gobshites, heard of 'em? Any good? Aye. They're a Celtic punk band from Massachusetts, so naturally they've got a good following. They've just released a new album, the bartender says. It's called "Give Ireland Back to the Irish." "The best Irish music is rebel music," they all agree. I don't really have an opinion on the matter, so I stay out of it. I wouldn't want to help things go wrong any faster than they're already supposed to.

Quencher Tavern

170 I St., South Boston
Phone: 617-269-9555

In For A Pound is Richard Marinick's 2007 novel set in Southie. It's about—what else—hard-headed criminals and corruption in the blue collar town. In one passage a character is leaving the Quencher:

"Wacko stared at the closed St. Peter's school on the corner, like most empty buildings in Southie, soon to be converted into condos. He made a face. 'Fucking yuppies,' he said. 'Fucking yuppies and feds, all we got over here in Southie these days.'"

I know how he feels. There's a squadron of realtors roaming around the block outside the bar studying their listings when I'm walking up. Later on I follow that same path Marinick describes on my way out of here thinking about his words and the words of the old Irish bartender at the bar. "How long has this place been here?" he said, repeating my question. "Forever."

"Since the turn of the century anyway. It used to be an apartment here." The Quencher, or Nino's Casino as regulars call it, is a skinny little bar room sliced out of the middle of a row of triple deckers like a long dash breaking up a sentence. Robert "Nino" Sances bought the place with his partner Joseph "Dodo" Nee back in 1982. They grew up in the neighborhood and were firefighters together in the city. The bar room used to be Nino's aunt's house.

"Across the street there you had the barber, that was still there. Next door was the butcher, and then the grocer and the seamstress." Further up there's the school. Then there's the church at the top of the hill. It's no wonder blocks like this in cities like this were insular for so long.

"You had everything you need," the bartender told me.

No one is satisfied simply inhabiting the block they grew up on anymore. I happen to think that's a good thing. Provincialism doesn't serve anyone well, especially the ignorant to the world at large sort. But there's something to be said for a close knit neighborhood. They've still got an approximation of that here at the Q. An entirely familiar crowd, each regular makes an appearance through the door like a familiar sit com character hitting their entrance cue. I bump into an old bartender from Cambridge I used to know who's working for the telephone company now.

"You don't see many places like this anymore," I offer, gesturing to the walls covered with mismatched signs, video screens, old fraying posters and the like. "Where I work in Roxbury you do," he says. "It's nice here, but it can get a little rough." This guy is like 6'2, 240 lbs. I'd hate to see just what it is he considers rough. I try to buy a round, but he's on the wagon he says. A lot of people in here seem to be. Some are taking a break, some gave it up for good. This is just the place they want to be anyway. It's what they know.

Meanwhile a few women are by the back door unloading bags of clothes onto the bar. They're talking about sizes with the bartender. I get the impression there's an impromptu sale going on here, but I don't exactly go poking my nose in to find out.

They leave through the back entrance. Eventually I follow out that way myself. It's like another world out here. Grassy yards stretching for blocks and blocks in between towering homes framed by the skeletons of wooden porches. You could sprint across the roofs here from house to house without stopping until you got winded. Keep running till the end of the known universe.

Touchie's Shamrock Pub

501 E 8th St., South Boston
Phone: 617-268-0007

Dive Bar Rating

Touchie's represents my 65th dive bar in the course of writing this book, and there are still a few things I haven't exactly figured out yet. Like when the right time to go to a dive to enjoy a relaxing beer is exactly. You'd think 1 am would be prime time for drunken shenanigans, and easy enough to avoid, but that would be operating under the rules of normal bar behavior. Dives operate on a different schedule altogether. It's like when you first start working the night shift and you get to see the city at sleep on your way to and from work. Or when you're on your way home from an ill-fated all-nighter at 8 am and you're watching normal people go about their normal business. What are these people doing? This doesn't seem right. Time takes on a thickness, it's harder to swim through. Same theory at work at Touchie's on a Thursday afternoon. It's an alternate dimension. Sixty year old men are wobbly-kneed and screaming at full throttle about purgatory at one end of the bar. What looks like a sewing circle is occupying a couple tables at the other end, quietly chatting over a few Bud Lights. I think I see my dead grandfather drinking in the corner by the video games. I've passed through the mirror into the ghost world here.

The bar is right on the edge of the old Boston harbor in a picturesque section of Southie. At the foot of a dense residential hill, thick with triple deckers, it's on the first floor of a residence. It smells of the ocean and family.

Inside it's the dive of your dreams. Yellow walls clashing with a green bar top. Ornate mosaic tiles cover the underside of the bar. The linoleum floor is cracked and peeling. There's a grill and a meat slicer behind the bar, an old timey coffee pot and an unused fryer; they serve lunch here till 4 every day. These objects seem threatening somehow. Behind that a window overlooks a tall condo building on the edge of the water. There's a grassy yard out front where the residents are walking their dogs. I watch them though the window while I watch the drinkers on either side of me at the bar watch me watching them. The voyeuristic set up is like a snake eating its own tail, only of far less consequence.

There's no more purgatory anymore, apparently, the preacher is yelling. It's hard to decipher this whiskey prophet's ramblings, but safe to assume the general gist of it is that we're all fucked. As the sun rises high in the sky over the building across the street the bartender closes the curtain over the window behind the bar. The dog walkers disappear from view. Now it's just the dim light from the overhead bulbs and the glowing TVs. Not sure if he's shutting out the world or shutting us all in.

On my way out I almost stumble into a pair of twenty something joggers hustling past the bar. I stand there and watch them for a minute as they rise up and over the hill and soon they're gone. Another duo follows right behind them as I cross the street. Then another.

Tom English's Cottage

118 Emerson St., South Boston
Phone: 617-269-9805

When outsiders are stereotyping Boston, what they are really talking about is South Boston. Parochial, insular, and suspicious of authority. Blue-collar, devotedly Catholic, vaguely racist, drunk and violent people obsessed with the ability of millionaire twenty five year olds to move a ball around. All of that is a gross stereotype as well. And if it were ever an accurate description at one point, it wouldn't even be the domineering stereotype of the current Southie. In fact it's become exactly the opposite in the past decade as gentrification has forced many of the families who lived here for generations to give way to condos, boutique restaurants and yuppie watering holes.

But there are still places like Tom English's, a bar that found itself the center of a racist shit storm a few years back over a collection of stuffed monkeys behind the bar that were allegedly set up to celebrate black history month. Old stereotypes die hard. The black guy who stole my seat at the bar when I went to take a piss here certainly couldn't care less about the bar's "racist" history, real or imagined or otherwise.

"I've got to teach these young girls how to pick the music," his friend croaks. It's the first thing I hear when I walk in. A deep, guttural mossy foghorn blast, like a battle-scarred drill sergeant with a throat cancer voice box; a familiar tenor in real Boston dives. The old feller is hugging a young lady of about fifty from behind by the neck and she's laughing it off. "Rock Lobster" is pumping on the jukebox, so I ascertain the source of his discontent pretty quickly.

"I chose poorly," she tells me when the salty ogre meanders off to the bar to freshen up his glass. He's got the gate of a navy man, an old vocation that I later verify from his bar stool pontificating.

"No way, I like the B-52s" I tell her.

"Yeah," she says, stammering, surveying the room with her eyes, then encompassing the entirety with a sweep of her head. "But you've got to consider the fucking population." That's pretty good advice in any bar come to think of it.

The population on a Thursday night is a phalanx of sturdy thick necks draining bottles in front of the Sox game. It's spacious in here, room enough for five times this crowd. A long, broad room with a twenty seater bar. The other side of the room is filled with booths and two pool tables.

I sit next to the B-52s fan and her friend. They're both dressed in untucked button down shirts, over-sized and billowy, topped off with flowing scarves. It's about 70 degrees out.

"I need the Kinks!" the second good time broad screams out as "Lola" comes on. The first is inching her foot across the bar stool in between us toward me before she gets scolded for being inappropriate. Hmmm... might make a good story for the book, I think, looking her over. Never mind. I'm not that dedicated. A silent old golem at at nearby table is taking stock. He's frozen, stuck to his seat, stuck in time. Inertia and booze are double teaming him. Double teaming us all in here. We talk for twenty minutes about the Celtics and Bruins later on. I couldn't turn away from him. Literally. Every time I tried he kept on talking as if I was still there.

The gang at the bar is rowdy, using their outside voices. There's no such thing as an indoor voice in a South Boston dive, unless, of course, you're talking about dirt—your own, or someone else's.

I'm expecting more of a crush of youthful drinkers any time now. They spill out of their apartments lined up and down newly fashionable East Broadway into the slew of bars like this on the Ave. They deaden themselves here with booze, then piss and fight and fuck their way back into life.

The Shannon Tavern

558 E 3rd St., South Boston
Phone: 617-269-9460

Dive Bar Rating

🍾🍾🍾🍾🍾

The lights are blazing in here. Like a row of arena-grade stage lights hanging in a straight column from the gold-tinted drop tile ceiling. Walking in from the heavy dusk of a Sunday evening it's a jarring transition. Sound-wise I'm struck as well. Aside from a persistent dog yelping away at nothing, the block is still. Inside the Shannon, a first floor tavern that's been in operation since 1960 on this residential block, the crowd is boisterous. Why not? It's Sunday.

There's a group at the bar yelling into their beers. One guy in full Celtics regalia has a killer bloody nose. He either just got punched in the face or pulled back a giant zinger that his sinuses didn't agree with. He's bullshitting loud and strong through it anyway, trying to get a story out. His friends won't let him. "You're a big fucking gay baby!" one of them tells him. Tells the whole neighborhood actually, considering his volume. The woman with them is decked out in a pink track suit and drinking white wine on the rocks out of a large Dunkin Donuts iced coffee cup.

I can't make out the rest of what they're talking about. What is that language? Irish? Is that even a language? I take my seat at the bar and am confronted with a telling sign. "God made liquor so the Irish couldn't rule the world."

Seated next to me are a quiet 70 something couple draining a pitcher of Bud Light and watching the Amazing Race on the tube. I'm in the corner by the deli lunch counter kitchenette. They serve food here during the day. "Sandwiches, chicken fingers, shit like that," the young bartender tells me. There's a pack of hot dogs and a giant tub of bleu cheese dressing in the fridge in front of me. Shitty food never looked so good. Four or five Miller Lights will do that to a man.

Pearl and her boyfriend Bobby grew up near here. I'm sitting next to Pearl and she has to relay everything I say to Bobby, then carry his reply back over to me. It's like a drunken game of telephone.

"Yeah, there's a lot of new people in the neighborhood." They're as sweet a couple as you're going to meet in a place like this. Bobby may or may not be mentally disabled, but he's a joker. Keeps going to shake my hand then pulling it away and laughing a big laugh that makes me smile on the inside.

"The bar's been here ninety years," he says. He's seen a good majority of them.

"This is a good place," Pearl agrees. "We drink here all the time. There's no trouble or nothing now either."

They both try to come up with some bars nearby that I might like. The Playwright, The Boston Beer Garden. Newer places. Shinier places. Part of young Southie. They don't seem to get that this is exactly the type of place I'm looking for.

Hipster warning

Best dives to show off your new ink

Aside from drunk Catholics, disenfranchised minorities, and swarms of nerds who'll be ruling the world one day, the other thing we've got a lot of in Boston is hipster pussies. Here are the dive bars you'll find them at.

The Model Cafe

Silhouette Lounge

Deluxe Cafe

Wally's Cafe

The Cantab Lounge

Charlie's Kitchen

P.A.'s Lounge

Rosebud Bar and Grill

Great Scott

Shea's Tavern

266 West Broadway
No phone

Dive Bar Rating

🍾🍾🍾

This afterthought of a bar on the main thoroughfare of Southie is attached to the back of a package store, so don't be surprised to find it crowded by unloaded boxes of beer and wine along one side of the room. A bar/storage room then, and a pretty good example of what I've come to know as the dive bar mirage. When you first walk into an unfamiliar dive, especially a strictly locals one like this, it's a pretty good idea to keep your head down and not look anyone in the eye. Dive bar drunks are like crocodiles or rhinos or whatever. Best not to show any outward signs of aggression if you don't want to get eaten.

The two guys drinking in here when I came in were covered in tattoos and looked pretty menacing. Your brain fills in the cracks with preconceived stereotypes when it doesn't have enough information, so I immediately cast them in the role of Southie toughs. Woops. Turns out they were were wearing flip flops and shorts and had ear plugs. Boy was I off on that one. No way you're gonna catch a beef from a guy in flip flops. After a whiskey or two it turned out that, just like anywhere else, they just wanted to shoot the shit about the Sox game. The TV was propped up on the end of the bar. None of that fancy wall-hanging business in here.

Over the course of the game a parade of neighborhood regulars strolled passed the open front door, poked their head in and asked what the score was. It feels like Shea's is a place people just need to pop into for a minute to make sure it's still here. A sketchy tweaker floats through asking for some napkins. A cute Irish waitress with a fresh brogue comes by after her shift to say hi to no one in particular. A woman in a Tampa Bay Rays hat screams something about baseball. I step outside for a smoke to get a little distance from the dive bar office hours. The building next door I stand in front of is a high end hair salon closed for the night. There's a disco ball spinning for no one in the middle of the ceiling.

When I come back in I notice there's a pristine red scooter parked in the middle of the bar amidst the unsorted inventory. The packie delivers, Frank the friendly old Irish bar man tells me. What's with the boxes Frank? "You should have seen the place when I got in today. I couldn't even get to the windows to open the blinds." The people need their beer. Especially around here I suppose. Sometimes you need a guy on a Vespa to deliver a 30 pack to your apartment too. Tell him to take a left at the disco ball.

Best of the Rest

Whether for space issues, or because they just weren't divey (or good at being divey) enough, these are some other worthy contenders that didn't make the final cut.

J & J Irish Pub & Grille, 1130 Dorchester Ave., Dorchester
A good example of how even the most spotless and well organized of bars can still scream out dive by the hang dog expression beneath the facade.

Shay's Pub and Wine Bar, 58 JFK St., Cambridge
Dim basement atmosphere with low ceilings, dusty pipes you can bang your head on, awful bathrooms, and English ale on tap.

Doyle's Cafe, 3484 Washington St., Jamaica Plain
Old historical bar has seen its share of historical figures come through since 1882, and has the scars to prove it.

Conor Larkin's Grill & Tap, 329 Huntington Ave., Boston
People think you're going to get weird looks when you walk into a lot of the locals-only dead-in-their-seats dive bars, but it's really the young, sporty basement dives like this Northeastern haunt where you'll find people with looking problems.

Williams Tavern

79 W. 2nd St., South Boston
No phone

This long, thin, lunch-counter-style bar, is plopped down in a punchy little brick building that looks like an undersized boxer with a chip on his shoulder and a broken nose. The three long window slits cut out of the wall are covered in metal wire, but they seem designed for a squadron of archers to fire off arrows at the advancing hoards. That's not as far fetched as it sounds, metaphorically anyway. A bar like this in Southie, or anywhere, has to have a strong defensive game to stave off defeat. Predictably, I found the building up for sale on a few different real estate websites when I digging around for details.

Perhaps they'd be doing a little better if they didn't keep such odd hours. I came by at eight o'clock on a recent Thursday night to find the place closed for the night. Around seven on another night I find a handful of patrons polishing off the last of a long day's worth of cold ones at the bar. There's a diner next door connected to the bar room. They're only open until 3, but if you prefer to sit in here with a drink the bartender will reach over through a slat in the wall to get your order. "We serve breakfast all day," the cute old bar lady tells me. "You can get whatever you want, chicken, turkey. It's good food at a good price too!"

I start to cough up a little bit of the steamy summer street dust, and all of the other older women down the bar kick into boozy matron mode. "Get him a drink! He's all scratchy!" one of them yells. Good idea, lady. Mine's a frosty Bud Light this time. (This dive bar trek has ruined my taste in beer). The bartender serves it with a tissue plugged into the top like an anarchist den mother handing me my very first molotov cocktail. Um, so what's that all about? "Some people like it in case they want to wipe the rim," she tells me. "Just in case cardboard or whatever gets in there." That had not occurred to me.

So who are the people who want to wipe the rim of their beer here? "Oh, it's lots of locals. It's a working bar," she says. "UPS, Post Office workers. People come in and have a beer after work before heading off closer to wherever they live."

Some of the ladies have started noticing my tattoos, so they ask for a closer look. What's the "47" on my arms mean, they want to know. "It's just my lucky number," I tell them. "My dad made me promise never to get one," Sandra tells me. She's about fifty five, looks like she's here for the long haul. "When you get old you'll be dragging your ass. It's all gonna look like 'blaaaa'" she cautions. "Sex will start looking like six..." Maybe, but who gets a "sex" tattoo anyway.

"I got my niece money for her birthday and she went out and got a tramp stamp! Now I said I'm just gonna give her gift cards from now on."

I tell her by the time my generation is old, so many people will have tattoos we'll all be able to look gross together. Also, does her niece plan on stopping in here anytime soon? You know, just so I can get an accurate description of the tattoo. For science.

"It's all about markings," she says, which sounds vague, but is definitely true. We all just want to mark ourselves as having belonged to something, whether it's a stupid in-joke amongst friends about the number 47 or a neighborhood bar.

INDEX

Ace's High, 188
Aga's Highland Tap, 166
Anchovies, 30
The Bar Room, 32
Beacon Hill Pub, 34
Biddy Early's, 36
BK's, 150
Black Horse Tavern, 38
The Boyne Pub, 12
Bus Stop Pub, 14
The Cantab Lounge, 74
Casey's, 172
Centre Bar, 110
Charlie's Kitchen, 76
Chelsea Walk Pub, 136
The Connection, 190
Corner Café, 96
Corner Pub, 40
Cornerstone Pub, 194
The Corner Tavern, 192
Cottage Tavern, 152
Courtside Restaurant and Pub, 78
Croke Park/ Whitey's, 196
Delux Café, 42
The Dot Tavern, 112
The Drinking Fountain, 154
Dublin House, 114
The Dugout, 44
Durty Nelly's, 98
The Eagle, 46
Eddie C's, 138
The Eire Pub, 122

El Mondonguito, 168
Fasika, 174
Four Winds Bar and Grille, 100
Galway House, 156
Hogan's Run, 16
JJ Donovan's, 50
JJ Foley's, 51
JJ Foley's Fireside Tavern, 158
Joey's, 18
Joey Mac's, 80
Kiley's Tavern, 198
The Last Drop, 20
Lower Mills Pub, 124
Midway Cafe, 160
The Model Cafe, 22
Murphy's Law, 200
Newtowne Grille, 82
Old Sully's, 102
On the Hill Tavern, 176
P.A.'s Lounge, 180
Paddy's Lunch, 84
Parrotta's Alpine Lodge, 140
Pat "Packy" Connors Tavern, 169
Peggy O'Neils, 126
The Penalty Box, 52
Portugalia, 86
The Pub, 178
Pugliese Bar & Grill, 88
Punter's Pub, 54
Quencher Tavern, 202
Red Hat Cafe, 55
Remmingtons, 56
Riverside Pizza, 90

Robyn's Bar and Grill, 62
Rosebud Bar and Grill, 182
Shangrilla Chinese Restaurant, 58
The Shannon Tavern, 208
Shea's Tavern, 210
Sidebar, 62
Silhouette Lounge, 24
Sligo Pub, 184
Sonny's Adams Village Restaurant and Lounge, 127
Sullivan's Pub, 104
Sullivan's Tap, 64
The Tam, 66
Tavern At the End of the World, 107
Taverna Medallo, 142
TC's Lounge, 68
Tom English Bar, 128
Tom English's Cottage, 206
Touchie's Shamrock Pub, 204
Trainor's Café, 144
Twelve Bens, 130
Upstairs Downstairs, 132
Victory Pub, 146
Wally's Cafe, 70
Williams Tavern, 212
Whitney's Cafe, 92

MORE BEST OF THE REST

Clerys, 113 Dartmouth St., Boston
A dive bar in frat boy's clothing.

Corrib Pub, 201 Harvard St., Brookline
A sign above the old fashioned cash register announces the date you must have been born on to drink legally. Probably doesn't get much use here I'm guessing.

Castlebar Pub, 575 Washington St., Brighton
One time Brighton area classic dive that's become a little too improved upon and collegiate.

Blackthorn Bar, 471 W. Broadway, South Boston.
Is it a dive or just an Irish pub? I've asked myself that 500 times this year, and with this one I still can't tell.

The Avenue Bar and Grille, 1249 Commonwealth Ave., Allston
Has all the trappings of a dive under the surface, but a few too many fancy touches to go all in.

Seven's Ale House, 77 Charles St., Boston
Almost anything would seem like a dive on Charles Street.

Hong Kong At Faneuil Hall, 65 Chatham St., Boston
Multi-level dance club – dive bar hybrid burned down in 2010, and just reopened. Huge fires have a way of ruining a bar's old character.

All Asia, 335 Massachusetts Ave., Cambridge
Slouchy, sticker-covered rock club is moving to a nicer spot soon

Phoenix Landing, 512 Massachusetts Ave., Cambridge
Plenty of puke and soccer fans ripping lines, but also sort of a real techno club, so...

Jeanie Johnston Pub, 144 South St., Jamaica Plain.
A little too Jamica Plainy.